D0203525

A Bibliography of John Rastell

A Bibliography of John Rastell

E.J. Devereux

SAINT LOUIS UNIVERSITY

OCT 27

WITHDRAWN

PR
2336
.R4
Z54
1999

McGill-Queen's University Press
Montreal & Kingston • London • Ithaca

© McGill-Queen's University Press 1999
ISBN 0-7735-1841-X

Legal deposit second quarter 1999
Bibliothèque nationale du Québec

Printed in Canada on acid-free paper

This book has been published with the help of a grant from the Humanities and Social Sciences Federation of Canada, using funds provided by the Social Sciences and Humanities Research Council of Canada.

McGill-Queen's University Press acknowledges the financial support of the Government of Canada through the Book Publishing Industry Development Program for its activities. We also acknowledge the support of the Canada Council for the Arts for our publishing program.

Canadian Cataloguing in Publication Data

Devereux, E.J. (Edward James), 1935-1994
     A bibliography of John Rastell
     Includes bibliographical references.
     ISBN 0-7735-1841-X
     1. Rastell, John, d. 1536—Catalogues. 2. Bibliography—Early printed books—16th century. I. Title.
     PR2336.R4Z54   1999
      015.421   C98-901127-5

It would be most fitting to dedicate this book, in Jim's name,

to the comradeship of scholarship,

to the loyalty of friendship,

to the efforts and perseverance of

Jane Toswell, Peter Auksi, David Bentley and Alan Somerset,

and of many other members of the English Department

of the University of Western Ontario.

Joan Devereux
Epiphany 1998

CONTENTS

PREFACE

When he died in January 1994 Jim Devereux was working on a study of Whitchurch and Grafton, having set aside the completed typescript of his bibliography of John Rastell for consideration at a later date. His efforts to publish the bibliography had been unsuccessful, in large part because, as an old-fashioned bibliographer, he had typed the necessary descriptions and collations on an old manual machine and made corrections by hand. Since he did not wish to commune with a computer, he left the project to one side until some solution presented itself. After his death, his widow Joan and his four children, Joanna, Cecily, Jeremy, and Benet, entrusted the typescript to Peter Auksi and Jane Toswell. The Faculty of Arts, in the person of the dean, James Good, and the Department of English—chair, Paul Gaudet—both strongly supported a successful application for a Social Sciences and Humanities Research Council Internal Research Grant. With those funds we were able to employ John Wooden, then a graduate student, to type this material into a DOS-simulation program that would readily upload into a formatting or typesetting program on a mainframe computer. Dr Wooden accomplished this task in the summer of 1994 and subsequently proofread the DOS file against the typescript. Over the winter of 1994-95 the book was uploaded successfully into a typesetting program that could, more or less, encompass the complexities of the layout and typographic characters. In this work Gerard Stafleu of the Information Technology Services at Western was invaluable. During this time many of the bibliographic entries were checked or augmented by Peter Auksi, Allan Gedalof, Richard Firth Green, Stanley H. Johnston Jr, Alan Somerset, Fiona Somerset, Jane Toswell, Paul Werstine, and A.M. Young. In the summer of 1995 most of the original photographs were located and the introduction was expanded with new material discovered in Jim's files by Joan Devereux. This material was incorporated into the manuscript by David Bentley and

Richard Shroyer under the auspices of the Canadian Poetry Press at Western. More formatting of the entries and updating of the references took place in 1995-96, and Peter Auksi produced a new bibliography of publications on Rastell. Jeremy Devereux obtained preliminary permission to publish from the relevant libraries, as listed below. Ian Doyle helped to arrange the photograph from Durham and provided useful information about Rastell publications. We were also heartened along the way by John Milsom, who expressed interest in the project and provided us with proofs of his "Songs and Society in Early Tudor London" *Early Music History* 16 (1998 for 1997), pp. 235-93. This article confirms many of Jim's conclusions, and raises other interesting, and persuasive, points about his use of music types, but it arrived too late to be addressed in detail in the book. The camera-ready copy was produced with the assistance of the facilities, including scanners, of the Canadian Poetry Press.

We would like to thank the following libraries for permission to publish materials from their collections:

Bodleian Library, University of Oxford for Bodleian Malone 22, title page and printer's device; Bodleian Douce frags. e. 38, opening of text; Bodleian Crynes 868(1); 8° F 1 Jur, title page, printer's device, and colophon; Bodleian Douce add. c. 2, title page and four other pages; Bodleian Mason Z 163, title page; Bodleian Douce M 739, errata and paste-in; Bodleian Vet A.1.d.2., page of text; and Bodleian Douce H.2.2., table of affinity.

By permission of The British Library, the following materials: BE 11/1 *Abridgement of Statutes* Father of Heaven, explicit with privilege; C.15.c.6 *Pastyme of People* pp. Ci, E7, L5, f5v; C.33.e.41 More, *Life of Pico*, title page with colophon; C.39.b.17 *Interlude of the Four Elements*, title page, music; C.40.g.2 *Terms*, opening of text; C.54.k.9 Littleton, *Tenures*, printer's device; C.65.aa.13 *Abridgement of Statutes* (1527) , last page of text with colophon and privilege; C.122.f.5 *Liber Assisarum*, frontispiece woodcut, woodcut after index and before text, title page and explicit, printer's devices; C.189.c.13, *Boke of the new cardys,* p. ai; G.7569 Linacre, *Progymnasmata* colophon, title; Harleian 5937 Thibault, *Prognostications*, title page with colophon; Huth 31 *100 Merry Tales*, title page, privilege; K.8.k.8 (Music Library) "A wey mornynge" printer's device.

By permission of the Syndics of Cambridge University Library, the following photographs are reproduced: Cambridge, Syn. 5.52.2, title page and printer's device; Cambridge, Syn. 5.55.2, page of text, woodcuts and printer's device.

University Library, University of Durham and the Trustees of Lord Crewe's Charity gave permission to reproduce Bamburgh Select 111, detail from fol. D4v.

The Folger Shakespeare Library gave permission to publish the errata-page from Thomas More's *Dialogue of Heresies* (STC 18084). The title page illustration from Skelton's *Against a comely Coystrowne*, Huntington 59200, and the letter-press title from *Pastime of People*, Huntington 82498, are both reproduced by permission of The Huntington Library, San Marino, California.

Niedersächsische Staats- und Universitätsbibliothek Göttingen for 4° Fab. Rom. IX, 150 Rara., colophon.

We are also grateful to the King's College Library, Cambridge and the Houghton Library at Harvard University for their willingness to help with permissions and identification of materials.

Since the completion of Jim's work, the indexers of the revised *Short Title Catalogue* have suggested some possible additions to Jim's descriptions. Since we are unable to submit these to the rigorous analysis that the other entries in this bibliography received, we have listed them in an appendix, along with a note by Alan Somerset commenting on some of these items. We hope that Jim would approve of the slight revisions which have updated his work here, and we know that he would agree with us that a critical bibliography of Rastell publications is a desideratum in the field of Tudor bibliography. We are particularly grateful to Joan Devereux for her help at every stage in the necessarily long process of preparing this manuscript for publication.

Peter Auksi

M.J. Toswell

Feast of St Bartholomew 1998

ACKNOWLEDGMENTS

Most people involved in the study of early sixteenth-century bibliography sooner or later become intrigued by John Rastell. His many interests and enthusiasms, his use of his press for his own idealisms, and his inevitable role in the shadow of his brother-in-law Thomas More all give him an appeal as human as it is historical. One can easily become tedious on the number of Rastell's ideas that made others famous, such as books of sermons for ignorant clergy, trade rather than plunder in the New World, a theatre in Finsbury where London citizens took healthy walks, and the use of the press to raise the moral vision of the people. Rastell is repetitive enough about these matters; I leave him to speak for himself as much as I can.

For the completion of this work, which has gone on for a very long time, I must thank my wife Joan, and our four children, Joanna, Cecily, Jeremy, and Benet, who have all been as forbearing as anyone could be over many years, my colleagues in the English Department at the University of Western Ontario, and two American colleagues whom I met late in the process, Professor Albert J. Geritz and Professor Amos Lee Laine.

Naturally I must also thank Katherine Pantzer, without whose help no work of this kind could ever be done. My thanks are also due to the librarians who gave me access to their collections or written replies to my inquiries, and especially those of the British Library, the Bodleian Library, the Cambridge University Library, the King's College Library and Pepys Library at Magdalene College, both in Cambridge, Balliol College Library in Oxford, Göttingen University Library, the Henry E. Huntington Library and Art Gallery, and the Folger Shakespeare Library.

For generous financial help in compiling all this information I am grateful to the Canada Council, the Social Sciences and Humanities Research Council of Canada, and the Faculty of Arts of the University of Western Ontario for grants in aid of research.

The bibliographical descriptions in this study follow the models of Fredson Bowers' *Principles of Bibliographical Description* (Princeton, 1949). Type identifications follow F.S. Isaac's *English and Scottish Printing Types 1501-35 * 1508-41* (London, 1930).

E.J. Devereux

ABBREVIATIONS

Arber   *A Transcript of the Registers of the Stationers' Company of London, 1554-1640* ed. Edward Arber. 4 vols, London, 1975-1994.

Beale   J.H. Beale, *A Bibliography of Early English Law Books* Cambridge, Massachusetts, 1926.

Cowley   J.D. Cowley, *A Bibliography of Abridgements, Dictionaries and Indexes of English Law to the Year 1800* London, 1932.

Dibdin   *Typographical Antiquities* Begun by Joseph Ames, augmented by William Herbert, and completed by T.F. Dibdin. 4 vols, London, 1810-1819.

Duff   E.G. Duff, *A Century of the English Book Trade* London, 1905.

Gibson   R.W. Gibson, *St. Thomas More, a Preliminary Bibliography of His Works and of Moreana to the Year 1750* New Haven, 1961.

Greg   Sir Walter W. Greg, *A Bibliography of the English Printed Drama to the Restoration* 4 vols, London, 1939-1959.

Hodnett   Edward Hodnett, *English Woodcuts 1480-1535* London, 1935. Reprinted with additions and corrections London, 1973.

Isaac   F.S. Isaac, *English and Scottish Printing Types 1501-35 * 1508-41* London, 1930.

L&P   *Letters and Papers, Foreign and Domestic, of the Reign of Henry VIII.* ed. J.S. Brewer, J. Gairdner, and R.H. Brodie. 21 vols, London, 1862-1932.

McKerrow R.B. McKerrow, *Printers' and Publishers' Devices in England and Scotland 1485-1640* London, 1913.

Reed   A.W. Reed, *Early Tudor Drama* London, 1926.

Roberts   R.J. Roberts, "John Rastell's Inventory of 1538," *The Library*, 6th series 1 (1979), pp. 34-42.

STC   A.W. Pollard and G.R. Redgrave, *A Short-title Catalogue of Books Printed in England, Scotland, and Ireland and of English Books Printed Abroad, 1475-1640* 2nd edition, begun by W.A. Jackson and F.S. Ferguson, completed by Katherine F. Pantzer. 2 vols, London, 1976-1986.

Introduction,

Typographical Preface

and

Book Designs

INTRODUCTION

John Rastell (c. 1475-1536) has always interested students of Tudor thought, from John Bale, who knew him late in life, to scholars of our own time, who have been bemused by the great variety of his concerns and the peculiar blend of idealism and opportunism that are so typical of his age and somehow also unique to him. Since his death, as during his life, he has been overshadowed by his friend and brother-in-law Sir Thomas More, a greater and wiser man no doubt, but a man who shared many of Rastell's interests and must have encouraged him in many of them, not least in the establishment of his press, the only European invention that is presented as of value in More's *Utopia*. That Rastell's press and his conduct of it repay study is clear, for no other printer of early Tudor England was as free as he to publish what he wanted, with only a slight regard for the demands of readers. He was in no way typical of the trade, and it is most unlikely that he knew a great deal about the craft or had any skill as a printer. But he was typical of a new middle class, with aspirations higher than mere success, and anxious to apply the new ideals of humanism to commerce, law, and trade. Even during the years around 1530, when his press earned him more than his legal work, the books that he printed were mostly written by his friends or himself. From the great legal publications that earned him his place in history down to his ruinous attempt to use the press to forward the English Reformation, he edited and printed books with an obvious sense that printing was something more than a trade. And his position as a lawyer and businessman not only made him more or less independent of what his press could earn but also gave him the freedom to publish what he thought would do good for the commonwealth. As he wrote in *Pastime of People*, his own history, "the crafte of Printynge of bokes began in the citye of Almayne, named Magonce whiche is nowe meruaylously increasyd, whiche hathe ben cause of great lernynge and knowelege, and hathe ben the cause of many thynges and great chaunges, & is lyke to be the cause of many straunge thynges here after to come."[1]

Rastell's idealism was almost utopian, yet his eye for the main chance during his lifelong search for honour and wealth was much more typical of his age. Clearly, like most other men in Tudor England, he saw no reason why he should not grow rich in a good cause and, especially during the 1520s, he was very prosperous. But he was heavily in debt in his last few years, when he tried desperately to get Thomas Cromwell to finance the publication of books against the old religion. If his reforming zeal did little to advance the new Church, it did bring him to the attention of the Pilgrimage of Grace, which demanded his arrest and the burning of his books. He had alienated his family, all of whom were shocked by his conversion and by the martyrdom in the previous year of Sir Thomas More. He had dissipated his fortune in bad investments and antagonized the ecclesiastical hierarchy by denying the legality of tithes, in the face of the Proclamation of 1535. Finally imprisoned "at the kynges own comandment," he lived miserably on "almys and charytie" until his death in 1536.[2] He was never brought from prison to trial, a terrible irony for a man whose writing on law and justice remained his greatest achievement. Old and lonely, he made his will, wrote a last letter to Cromwell, and died.[3]

Through a busy lifetime he had been many things: a lawyer, a coroner, a mathematician with a special interest in the use of arabic numerals, a printer or publisher in whose shop he or someone in his employ invented the method of printing music with a single impression, a public servant, a member of Parliament, an agent at court, an engineer in the French wars (and a decorator of pavilions for the Field of Cloth of Gold), one of the first and most important translators and codifiers of English law, a dramatist who wrote and produced interludes on his own stage (and was the first to publish English secular drama), a would-be colonizer of North America, an historian, and, at the last, a controversialist on the Catholic and—after a meeting with John Frith—the Protestant side of the English Reformation. Most of his contemporaries speak well of his abilities until late in his life, when he seems to have become at least mildly deranged, perhaps as much because of his muddled financial affairs as owing to his startlingly sudden conversion in religion. The young reformers accepted him as a convert, though with scant respect, while one of Cromwell's agents at the Charterhouse tried to have him kept from arguing with the monks, "for they laugh and jest at all things that he speaketh." When he made his will on 20 April 1536 he named as executors his neighbour Ralph Cressey and King Henry VIII, presumably a final gesture against the world which had found no place for his clear moral and legal imperatives.

Few printers in Tudor England had Rastell's freedom to publish what he wanted people to read, with only a secondary regard for the book market and an overwhelming concern to serve the commonwealth and show the greatness of the English language. From the important law books that earned him a respectable place in at least one branch of history down to his ruinous attempt to use his press to advance the cause of the English Reformation, he always edited and published books with an understanding that printing was more than just an improvement in the scrivener's art—it was also a way of spreading ideas to improve the world.

Rastell was often referred to as a Londoner, which may indeed be true, but his family was from Coventry,[4] where his father Thomas Rastell was a lawyer,[5] and he maintained ties with that city all his life.[6] Judging by the date of his enrolment in the Coventry Corpus Christi Guild, which normally occurred at the age of fourteen, he was probably born about 1475;[7] the Guild would have given him his lifelong interest in drama as well. He may have studied at Oxford, as Anthony Wood claims,[8] and he certainly studied at the Middle Temple, where he is referred to in 1502 as an utter (i.e. outer) barrister. At about the age of twenty he married Elizabeth, the daughter of John More;[9] by 1499 he was sufficiently affluent to provide security, with his wife's family, for a loan of a hundred marks. In 1506 he succeeded his father as coroner of Coventry,[10] where he was visited by his wife's brother, Thomas More, whose letters describe a meeting with a preaching friar. As A.W. Reed demonstrates in *Early Tudor Drama,* the Coventry years were busy and productive, a time in which Rastell made a name for himself as a lawyer and citizen, inherited money from a Joan Symonds (who had paid his fees in the Guild and acted as godmother to his daughter), and no doubt established some valuable friendships, including one with Sir Anthony Fitzherbert, whose *Grand Abridgment* was to be one of Rastell's most important books. It must have been during the same time that he formed his strong views on natural law and right reason, which to the end he asserted with more force than subtlety, and on justice for all under the laws of Nature, Man, and God. Whether he formed radical views on religion then, as Reed, perhaps hopefully, inferred, is doubtful; he could well have held a certain independence in religion and likely shared in the anticlericalism of some of the English middle classes of his time, but his devotion to law could just as well have led him to oppose the antinomian tendencies of Lollardy—insofar as there is any consistent body of thought that can be called that. When he wrote in favour of Purgatory in 1530, he affirmed it on the basis of natural law, in a dialogue without scriptural citations; neither the doctrine that he championed nor his avoidance of Bible texts suggests much affinity with the Lollard tradition.

In 1508-09 he resigned as coroner of Coventry and began moving his family to London, where he evidently continued legal work and set up a press in Fleet Street, at "the abbot of winchecombe his place." Presumably all this had been planned for some time, and the move was at least partly inspired by the accession of the young humanist, Prince Henry, "Henricum octauum seu potius Octauium," as Lord Mountjoy called him in his letter inviting Erasmus to England.[11] There was a sense of change, even of the beginning in England of a Golden Age, centered on the commercial power of London and the humanist prince. By the time he moved to London Rastell had already absorbed ideas and attitudes from the guildsmen and the humanists that were substantially democratic and almost egalitarian. Reed probably makes too much of Rastell's overseeing a will leaving English Bibles while he was still in Coventry, an act that could possibly be interpreted as evidence of radical sympathies and connections; More wrote later of allowed Bibles in English, and it is likely that any ordinary could permit individual copies. But it is most certain that Rastell went to London intent on a career that would advance the cause of humanity as much as it would advance his own, taking with him a deep faith in the improvement of everyday life through education and in the betterment of the human condition through understanding of divine, human, and natural law. He explained all this in the first prefaces, in the early law books, and not long before his death he sang his old song again to Archbishop Cranmer and Bishop Gardiner. All his views were similar to those of More; and indeed so much of Rastell can be found in *Utopia*—especially the practical application of humanist ideals to everyday life—that it can be surmised, albeit without proof, that More learned as much from Rastell as he taught him.

Since the Utopians, simplifiers of legal affairs and practical humanists that they were, admired only printing and papermaking among European inventions, Rastell focused on the utility of those innovations and soon developed ideas of the power of the press far different from those of earlier and contemporary stationers. Like so many other humanists at the time, Rastell must have hoped that the press would point the way for the beginning of a better world, open to new ideas and revaluations. He must have hoped that he could share in this new beginning through reforms in law and legal education, the service of the commonwealth, and the printing and dissemination of good English books to serve good causes. His first press in London, in Fleet Street at the Abbot of Winchecombe's place, provided an opportunity to put his ideas into practice.

The only book we know contained the Winchecombe Place imprint is More's translation of the life of Pico della Mirandola, written by Pico's nephew and published probably in 1509 or a year or so later. More seems to have done the translation some years earlier, probably in 1505, the year of his marriage, when he "propounded to himselfe, as a patterne of life, a singular lay-man Iohn Picus;" More dedicated it to his "sister in crist" Joyce Leigh, a poor Clare at the Minories, whose family were friends of the Mores.[12] The book includes three letters and some small works of devotion as well as the life. More probably intended it as a relatively simple compendium of Florentine Christian Neoplatonism. Very likely Rastell saw it as a guide to sanctity for laymen dealing with secular affairs. It is an attractive book, without ornament or display type, with the 93a textura which almost certainly was Rastell's first and, at the time, only, type used carefully and to lovely effect. The format is quarto in sixes, which Rastell also used for an edition of John Stanbridge's *Long Accidence* at about the same time.

Rastell's obviously temporary premises were on "the Wharff or common wey ioynyng to the South syde of Fletestrete," later valued at £6 by the Court of Augmentations.[13] Given the humanist bias of the publications, it seems possible that the lease was arranged through the abbot, Richard of Kidderminster, whose concern for the new learning was such that he was said to have developed Winchecombe into "altera noua vniuersitas."[14]

Fairly soon—1512 seems as good a guess as any—Rastell moved his press to another house at the south side of St Paul's Cathedral, beside Paul's Chain. Here he and his workmen, probably under the guidance of Thomas Bercula, began an ambitious series of legal publications, which were intended to serve the commonwealth by making the law more accessible, and no doubt to be a successful business venture at the same time. They are large books, for which a considerable stock of bastard type—more or less usual for law books—had to be either bought or cast, and a great deal of effort had to go into editorial work and indexing, much of which Rastell himself undertook. For these a fount of English bastard, very similar to those used by de Worde and the law printer Richard Pynson, was acquired, and Rastell's two devices, one humanist and the other legal, were cut and used together, while Rastell produced indexes and prefaces.

In 1512 Rastell was also in the service of Sir Edward Belknap, apparently as an engineer entrusted with moving artillery for the French War of that year. When the war ended two years later, he was called on to supervise the unloading into the Tower of London of eighteen hoys loaded with guns and ammunition. Presumably he had been doing such work for some time and was considered capable of the task; presumably also such engineering explains why John Bale and John Pits both later refer to him as a mathematician. Aside from the immediate benefits in payments and influence, Rastell also received through Belknap's intercession a grant of the wardship of Richard Hunne's daughters and the use of their estate. This grant, which came on 7 October 1515 (less than a year after Hunne died or was murdered in the Lollards' Tower), obviously gave Rastell working capital for his publications and for the planning of his later New World voyage, but it also led to a lawsuit in 1523, when he was supposed to have paid the girls' dowries.[15]

There seems no way to estimate how large Rastell's printing establishment had grown in the meanwhile; the Pico book was a family venture, which could have produced a return, while the Stanbridge book was presumably commercial. Whatever returns from the press were, the new shop at Paul's Chain was set up for large publications, planned as profitable contributions to a world of justice. Several books on specifically humanist concerns that belong to the Paul's Chain period (c. 1512-17) cannot be dated precisely, but the two large legal texts can be assigned to about 1514. The first of these, the *Liber Assisarum et Placitorum Corone*, is a compilation of the yearbooks and assize records from the reign of Edward III (1327-1377), not the longest reign in English history but one marked by the importance of Parliament and the Courts.

Rastell's prologue to the *Liber Assisarum* is a long and repetitive argument that law and the making of law are natural to mankind, which is not ordered by instinct or by the kind of natural law that governs irrational nature:

> To study and to lerne and to tech laws is a lyfe gode and verteous And ... to execut lawes treuly & iustely is an acte right good & meretoreious, wherfore I may conclud that by cause lawes of them self be gode and so grete good cometh thereof, The comon wel by al reson must rathir stand in augmenting & preferring of laws then other in riches power or honour so they that exersise & bysi the*m*self in making laws in ordering and writing of lawes in lerning of lawes or teching lawes or in iust & trew executing of laws be thos parsons that gretly oncres & multiply the come*n* welle.

Rastell's first published composition, this is an extended statement on the importance of law in human, and indeed divine, affairs, and is almost utopian in its intent. Unfortunately it is all too typical of his thought and writing; the tiresome repetitions and the tortuous logical demonstration of more or less self-evident points are characteristics that remained with him to the end of his life. Essentially, the long text merely states that law is natural to human affairs and necessary for orderly life, a point that Rastell would make time and time again.

Rastell was involved with others in the production of the *Liber Assisarum*—certainly Richard Pynson (the King's Printer) and Wynkyn de Worde, and possibly a group of lawyers as well (see Bibliography 3). Some two years after the publication of the *Liber Assisarum*, Rastell or his associates proceeded with the second of these legal texts, an extremely large work, Sir Anthony Fitzherbert's *Graunde Abridgment*, "conteyning .vi or vii C leuis of grete pap*er*," which was completed by 21 December 1516.

An interesting group of smaller books followed: an edition of Thomas Linacre's Latin grammar, which had just been rejected for use at St Paul's School by its founder, John Colet, the renowned theologian and humanist; a part of a monastic compilation organizing piety according to the parts of grammar in the traditional Donatus; *Fulgens and Lucrece* by Henry Medwall, the first printed English secular drama; and William Harrington's *Commendations of Matrimony*, written at the suggestion of Polydore Vergil. All the authors were friends of More, and all the books combined humane studies with moral guidance in the humanist manner, which is hardly surprising since More was writing *Utopia* at this time.

Possibly in anticipation of Rastell's intended expedition to the New World, the Paul's Chain shop wound down with the publication of Rastell's *Tabula* on 10 February 1517, after which Rastell made arrangements with the More family to handle his financial affairs on behalf of his wife and children. Like the wardships of Hunne's daughters and the lease Rastell took at about the same time on a house at Monken Hadley, near High Barnet, this arrangement was to lead to troublesome litigation in the 1530s.[16]

On 5 March 1516 [1517], Rastell and two associates, Richard Spicer and William Howtyng, received a letter of recommendation under the Great Seal from the King, describing them as travelling "pro certis Negotiis nostris & suis expendiendis, ad longinquas Mundi Partes," and requesting safe passage for themselves, their trade goods, and their tools and weapons.[17] The King's concerns about safe passage remain undefined, probably because they were nonexistent. However, when Rastell, Spicer, and Howtyng embarked on their expedition to Ireland and across the ocean, they encountered many obstacles despite Henry's safe conduct—most of which seem to have had the sanction of the lord admiral, the earl of Surrey. There were constant delays, frustrations, and pilfering of trade goods, and John Ravyn, purser of one of the three ships that sailed in the early summer of 1517, even led the other seamen in an attempt to turn the expedition into one of piracy. The more than thirty soldiers Rastell and his associates had been given did nothing to defend them or their goods. Finally Howtyng, aboard the *Mary Barking*, "was put and lokkyd in his cabban at the hauyn of kork in yreland," while Ravyn and another officer

> exortyd the seid Rastell...to gyff vp his viage & to fall to robbyng vppon
> the see & to take on henry mongan a mayster of a barke of yreland whych

> had takyn a portyngale shyp ther and seyd that he myght do it by the law
> of the see & that hit shuld be as profitable to hym as his fysshyng in the
> new londes.

Ravyn and Rastell finally parted company after an argument at the house
of Thomas Dryvam in the vicinity of Waterford, by which time the little
flotilla had been in many places without once venturing onto the western
ocean. The ships sailed away, leaving Rastell in Ireland, where he spent
two apparently prosperous years.[18]

In the background of Rastell's voyage and his brother-in-law's *Utopia*
lie some shared works, principally Martin Waldseemüller's *Cosmographiae Introductio*, which was published at Lisbon in 1507 with
Amerigo Vespucci's *Quattor Nauigationes* as an appendix. More even-
tually became ironic about Vespucci's ill-concealed rapacity; Rastell, on
the other hand, turned to a pragmatic idealism. To judge by Rastell's
Interlude of the Four Elements, which was probably printed in 1520,
shortly after his return from Ireland, the benefits he had sought from the
New World in his abortive expedition were simple: fish, lumber, soft-
wood pitch, and soap ashes. His trade goods included cloth in large quan-
tities, household utensils, and a few luxuries. The ships carried both
masonry and carpentry tools, clear evidence that he hoped to build some
kind of permanent settlement, perhaps a trading fort to be guarded by the
soldiers sailing with him, although they had shown their warlike nature
only in squabbles with the sailors. Certainly he had only peaceful intentions, and the *Interlude* shows that his plan was to head for the evergreen
forests and rich fishing grounds of the North, far away from the Spanish.[19]

Little is known about Rastell's life during the two years between the
beginning of the voyage and 1519, though his reference to Ireland's "holsome grounde" in the *Interlude*, his completion of that play and a translation of the Statutes bearing penalties, and the gusto with which after his
return he opened his third printing house, moved on to a life of remark-
able activity, and prosecuted Ravyn in the Court of Requests for disrup-
tion of his voyage and theft of his trade goods all imply that they were
good years. Moreover, by the end of 1520 he had two new books out,
both his own work, both outlining his constant theme of service to the
commonwealth, and both arguing the importance of writing and publishing books in English. As discussed in the "Typographic Preface" which
follows, both books are quite unattractive; whoever was doing Rastell's
printing for him at the time, it was certainly not the "Thomas Berculay of
london prynter some tyme seruante vnto master Rastell" who had gone
with him on the New World voyage. That talented printer had moved on
into the service of the King's Printer, Richard Pynson.[20]

As for writing of English, Rastell's messenger figure in the *Interlude* is even more emphatic than was Rastell in the preface to the Statutes translation, informing the audience that his author had often pondered

> What number of bok*es* in our tonge maternall
> Of toyes and tryffelys be made and impryntyd
> And few of them of matter substancyall
> For though many make bok*es* yet vnneth ye shall
> In our englyshe tonge fynde any wark*es*
> Of connynge that is regarded by clerk*es*.

Since the Greeks and Romans wrote in their own languages, the argument continues, so should the English:

> Consyderyng that our tonge is now suffycyent
> To expoun any hard sentence euydent
> They myght yf they wolde in our englysh
> Wryte workys of grauyte somtyme amonge.

Furthermore, there are "pregnaunt wytt*es*" [minds] who read only English, and many English books appear "of loue or other matter not worth a myte." The argument is abundantly clear: the use of English will spread knowledge and assert the dignity of the nation; knowledge is not only practically beneficial but moral, for the quest for knowledge makes everybody better; service to the commonwealth is more important than wealth or power, as had been asserted before in the law books from Paul's Chain; and, implicitly, learning the law of Nature will enable people to learn the law of man, and from that the law of God.

Between 1520 and late 1522 or so Rastell seems to have let his press stay more or less idle, leaving the shop as a place of sale in the hands of "Iohn Heron habberdasher."[21] During this period he worked on rebuilding his legal fortunes and also returned to the service of his old patron Belknap, who had been entrusted with building and decorating the Round House at Calais and the English showpiece at Guisnes, both vital to national prestige. From the spring of 1520 Rastell must have been very busy with his associates, for the work was behindhand and completion of these "greate and importunate charges" would have allowed little time for other things. Furthermore, he would have recently completed the prosecution of Ravyn. As a debtor to the Crown, he paid 250 marks in 1521, but failed to pay the 810 marks due in respect to the Hunne indentures at Michaelmas 1522, which led to forfeiture of Hunne's property to Roger Whaplode, who had married one of Hunne's daughters. Rastell, however, managed to hold off turning the property over to him for some years.[22]

Belknap died during 1521, but Rastell had by then established a reputation as a supervisor of public works. In 1522 he showed how effective he was with a pageant performed at the little conduit at the Stocks to greet the Emperor upon his entrance into London. This pageant, which has been studied by Sidney Anglo, was a mechanical depiction of the natural world of England—with artificial animals, birds, and flowers—in which images of the King and Emperor cast away their swords and embraced, causing "an ymage off the father of hevyn all in burnyd golde" to rise and bless them.[23] The pageant symbolized the three laws (divine, natural, and positive), and its setting recalls the more elaborate of the two printer's devices used by Rastell (see page xxx).

Despite the legal struggle with the Whaplodes, Rastell seems to have settled his affairs reasonably well by 1524, when he took a forty-year lease on land in Finsbury Fields and built not only a house but a stage for dramatic presentations, which he stocked with all-purpose players' costumes.[24]

In 1524 or 1525 the shop at Paul's Gate acquired a new tenant—Thomas Kele, a skilled printer with a group of associates who had been, like himself, apprenticed to Pynson.[25] Rastell had been writing and translating various works and, apparently, accumulating several printing projects. The ensuing three or four years saw a steady output of legal and humanist books: an English and Law French text of the *Old Tenures*, Rastell's very successful *Expositiones Terminorum Legum Anglorum* (also in English and Law French, "to expown certyn obscure and derke termys," for "he that is ignorant of the termys of any sciens must nedys be ignorant of *the* sciens"), a translation of Sir Thomas Littleton's *Tenures*, the first English jestbook and the comic *Jests of the Widow Edith*, as well as assorted small legal texts, poetry, religious writing, and an educational experiment. So busy, in fact, was the press that, even with skilled workmen, some work had to be farmed out to Peter Treveris in Southwark. Book design, like the book list, was fanciful, and in about 1525 the house was given the sign of the Mermaid, presumably taken from Rastell's larger device. Most books were still his own work or those of his close friends, including his edition of Lucian's *Necromantia,* which has More's Latin text and an English translation that sounds as if it were by Rastell himself. Indeed, there is a light-heartedness in the themes and typography of this series of smaller books, with their ornamental titles and colophons, that suggests both success and a love of good letters. Rastell and his friends were writing successfully, the printing house workmen were doing very nice work, some books were selling well (judging by the later inventory), and, despite setbacks at law, Rastell seems to have both prospered and risen in standing in both City and Court without aspiring to the dangerous heights attained by his brother-in-law More. This was presumably the time when, as he later wrote to Cromwell, his press earned him more than his pleadings at Westminster Hall.[26]

During the same years other visible and external signs of success and good position in the world appeared. Rastell seems to have held onto the Hunne estate until the end of the decade, despite the court decision in favour of the Whaplodes.[27] The marriage negotiations for Princess Mary in 1527 had him working on Court pageantry again, this time with Hans Holbein, in decorating and building at Greenwich.[28] He was busy as one of the lawyers authorized to examine and sign Chancery Bills of Complaint,[29] and in 1529 became a member of the Reformation Parliament for a Cornish borough, Duneved.[30] These and other concerns suggest not only that he had become a person of importance and even some influence but also that he was beginning to be influenced by Thomas Cromwell, then Cardinal Wolsey's indispensable servant but soon to become the leading force of the following decade.

Remarkably, both the choice of books for publication and the design or style of the books changed in late 1527 to 1528 to suggest a new *gravitas*, and the press at the Mermaid was redirected, as it were, to bring natural reason more strongly to bear on the religious and national problems that would have to be dealt with. The first book of this stage of Rastell's career was in some ways the most important, the *Dialogus de fundamentis legum Anglie et de conscientia*, a work universally attributed to Christopher Saint Germain and commonly known as *Doctor and Student*. This classic study of the relationship between English law and canon law was to become a significant text in the development of the English Reformation and is generally considered a landmark in the common law. The book's simplicity of design reinforces the weightiness of its subject.

There is a natural tendency to see the publication of *Doctor and Student* as marking some parting of the ways between Rastell and More; certainly it conveys a rather Erastian tone, and More was later to attack an author, seemingly unknown to him but now believed to be Saint Germain, in *The Debellation of Salem and Bizance* (STC 18081). But even though both Rastell and Saint Germain were to be used by Cromwell and Cromwell was to become the perhaps unwilling instrument of More's death, it must be remembered that Rastell had further things to say on the debate between the churches and for a year or two yet would be on More's side. Furthermore, while Rastell might have suggested to an old friend, which Saint Germain was, that his study could do more good in English than in the original Latin of the *Dialogus* and, moreover, that the readership might include many who were not themselves lawyers—and might also have connected Saint Germain with his own printing sub-contractor, Peter Treveris, who published the first two editions of the English second dialogue (STC 21565-21566)—still, Rastell's subsequent works and his own kindly approach to the young heretic John Frith show no real attachment to the attitudes scholars have found in *Doctor and Student*. At that stage of the English Reformation he could have published the book for a friend without agreeing with all of it; it is not impossible that Saint Germain was a friend of More as well.

In the first half of 1529, Rastell's plans to publish *Pastime of People*, a reasonable chronicle of England based on Fabyan and other sources, were interrupted by the need to print More's *Dialogue of Heresies*, an attack in English—and very vigorous English at that—on Martin Luther and William Tyndale, the first result of More's having been licenced to read heretical books for refutation. Because of More's penchant for revisions, printing for his in-law was troublesome, but Rastell clearly felt it worthwhile and he resolved to join More in reasoning against the new religion.[31]

In the meantime *Pastime of People*, the last product of Rastell's cultivated leisure, awaited completion and publication before Rastell could join battle. The *Pastime* was both new in its presentation and reasonable in its thought. The story of Albion and her sisters was rejected as a myth that made the English a laughing stock—"I meruayle i*n* my mynde *that* men hauyng any good naturall reason wyll to such a thi*n*ge gyue credence." Its design was intended to make all information easily available: all important names were looped within factotums [blank borders], all-purpose woodcuts were used to illustrate historical personages, sections were divided by rows of type ornament, and marginal letters on each page indicated the parts of history being treated. The two sections of the chronicle, history before and after the Conquest, seem to have been planned for separate sale to customers who did not want both. There was a letterpress title, presumably the earlier, and a xylographic one, presumably from the same workshop, that gave the second part of the book, with its full-page woodcuts of all the kings from William the Conqueror, its special appeal. It seems, from the post-mortem inventory, to have sold quite well.

While More's *Dialogue* and *Pastime of People* were passing through the presses of Rastell and Peter Treveris (who completed More's book), Rastell himself set to work on his dialogue on the doctrine of purgatory. The central issue in the purgatory debate was the reformed doctrine of justification by faith as developed and taught by Luther. Among the side issues in the debate were the traditional anti-clericalism of the mercantile classes (and perhaps the voiceless poor); the English nationalism that had been expressed in the statutes of praemunire (and was soon to be used effectively and seemingly with public approval against the clergy); and perhaps even a bourgeois feeling that abolishing purgatory would abolish a costly tax on souls. These issues had all been expressed with vigour and much oversimplification in Simon Fish's *Supplication for the Beggars,* probably in 1529, and answered with nothing short of outrage by More in *The supplycacyon of soulys*, published by William Rastell (John's son) before 25 October 1529.[32] John Fisher, the Bishop of Rochester, who would be More's fellow-martyr, had earlier written a defence of purgatory based on patristic texts, while More's was based mainly on scriptural evidence.[33] It seems almost inevitable that Rastell would elect to continue the debate with an argument based on the law of nature, which he had consistently seen as the self-evident reflection of the laws of God and of man.

Rastell followed More not only in asserting this traditional doctrine, but also in form, for *A new boke of purgatory* imitates the *Utopia* in its dialogue form, in its use of the meeting of a slightly muddled Christian European and a supremely logical non-Christian in an exotic market place, and in its development of a fictional world that shows the extent to which logic and a higher pleasure principle could lead towards the ideals of Christianity apart from the use of Scripture. Rastell lacked More's talents, and his book had neither the subtlety of language nor the deep insights of *Utopia.* Nevertheless *A new boke of purgatory* went to a second printing after its first appearance on 10 October 1530.

Rastell's erratic thinking on purgatory and his insistence that the point be argued without scriptural reference led with surprising rapidity to his conversion to the reformed religion. The young reformer John Frith was planning a response to More and Fisher from the relative safety of the Continent when a friend in England suggested that Rastell add an element of the ridiculous to the very serious argument. On receiving Rastell's book along with More's, Frith wrote in his preface to *A disputacion of Purgatorye,*

> I was meruelously desyrous & tickled to se what reasons he brought for his probacions. And in the begynninge and prologe of the boke, he sette seuen reasons whiche he sayed that fonde felowes alleged for them to proue that there coulde be no purgatorye. And in dede they are very fonde that wolde denye purgatorye, yf there were no better argumentes to confute it then he assigneth.

No reformer could possibly accept an argument that was not based on Scripture. Though Frith seems to have been trying to be charitable, he was under some pressure and poor Rastell became an easy victim to student wit. Unfairly but not inaccurately Frith describes him:

a prenter dwelli*n*ge at Pouwels gate in London and of Master Mores al-
lyaunce, which also coueteth to countrefayte his kynsman, althoughe the
beames of his braynes be nothynge so radyaunte nor his conueyaunce so
commendable in the yes of the wyse.[34]

Rastell's lost, second book on purgatory apparently accused Frith of flip-
pancy and disrespect, while More, whom Frith had treated much more
respectfully, responded with sharp sarcasm to "good yong father Frith."
    Leaving his press to the workmen who were doing statute printing and
to his son William, Rastell pushed on with the idealistic intention of sav-
ing Frith. On the back of a sheet pertaining to the lawsuit between Rastell
and the carpenter Henry Walton over the bill for Rastell's home stage
someone, presumably Rastell himself, has written a title: "The cause why
*tha*t Rastell made his boke off p*ur*gatory w*ith*out aleggyng any text*es* of
holy scripture," and a part sentence, "I m*ar*uell gretely that my broder
Fryth doth hold this. . . ."[35] This is probably all that remains of the second
book on purgatory, but its contents can be partly reconstructed from
Frith's reply to it. Whether Rastell printed it or not, the preface to Frith's
second book shows that he visited the young reformer in prison and
showed it to him:

Brother Rastell I thanke yow that it hath pleased you to be so fauourable
vnto me a pore presoner as to shewe me a copie of your boke which yow
haue wryten to confute my reasons & scrypture that I haue alleged against
purgatory, for that hath caused me to make a subsydy defence & bulwarke
to my boke which by goddes grace shalbe an occasion to open more lyght,
although not to yow, yet at the lest wyse vnto them whose hartes the prince
of this world hathe not blynded but that the lyghte of the gospell and glorye
of Chryste maye shyne in the*m*. And where as yow wryte & proteste that
yow wyll brenge no scripture agaynst me. But only rehersse my scrypture
againe whiche I haue alleged vnp*er*feytlye and wounde me with myne
owne dartes, & wyll but euen do as one that playeth at tennes wyth another
tossinge the balle agayne, I doo verye well admitte your similitude.

Taking up Frith's texts without presenting any of his own seems typical
of Rastell, as does the rather ponderous metaphor of tennis, to which
Frith could retort that "somtyme ye play a touch of legerdemayne & caste
me a ball which when it commythe I perceaue to be non of myne."[36]
    As well as indicating that Frith had not been able to acquire all of Ras-
tell's second book, *An other boke against Rastel* suggests that Rastell's
response had been maddeningly avuncular in tone, and, in this, indebted
to More's ironic treatment in *The Confutation of Tyndale's Answer* and
elsewhere of young men who took it upon themselves to challenge the

ancient consensus of Christendom and its elder guardians. As More wrote in the *Confutation*, ".iii. olde men, my brother Rastell, the bysshoppe of Rochester and I, matched wyth father Fryth alone, be now but very babys."[37] Apparently Rastell began by arguing that scriptural proofs could be left out of the dispute because there were those who did not believe and those who used scripture for their own purposes (for Frith such people were damned and need not be included in the dialogue), and warmed to his task by accusing Frith of self-conceit and denouncing his "raylynge and dispraysynge other" (Frith denied mocking anyone, "sauynge a lyttell gestyng"). Rastell then appears to have claimed that Frith would do away with good works. To this—a fairly common response to the Lutheran doctrine of justification by faith—Frith answered patiently, urging Rastell "to put on his spectacle, and loke agayne vppon my boke," and at one point arguing in a parodic syllogism, "because you are somewhat slow in perceyuing the matter."[38]

Whether they met again before Frith was burned as a heretic is not known, but it seems certain that by the end of 1532 Rastell had accepted the new religion and, indeed, had decided to dedicate his writing and his press to its advancement. These moves must have alienated him from his brother-in-law, who resigned the chancellorship and began writing a sequence of books against the reformers, and from his son William, who printed them as fast as More wrote them.

Rastell's conversion brought him only scant respect from the reformers. Such at least is the conclusion to be drawn from the embarrassment that he caused Cromwell's agents at the London Charterhouse and from the unflattering comparison with More and Bishop Fisher made by the anonymous editor of Frith's book against Rastell:

> Rastell had nothynge commen with them. But only many yeres & a wyt sophisticall whych he called naturall reason, as a pertaininge to goddes worde he aknowleged hymselfe ignoraunt therof notwithstondinge had such opinion of his wyt that he thought he coulde as well proue purgatory by it as the other .ii. hadde donne by the scryptures wherin I thynke he was not deceaued and as this iii were not like so toke they the answere made to them not a like, More & Rochester thought foule scorne (see what the glorye of this worlde & hygh estimacioun of our selfes doth) that a ionge man of smale reputacion shulde take vppon him so cleane contrarye to their opinion to writte agaynste them. And to be shorte toke the matter so greuously that they could neuer after be quyet in their stomakes vntyll they had dronken his bloud. Rastell though he perceyued his natural reason to be sore sayd to, yet was he not malicious as the other were. And therfore wrote he agayne, which work of Rastell came to his handes when he was presonner in the Tower of London, where he made the answer folowynge

to the same which answere after Rastell had reade, he was well content to
counte his natural reason folyshnes and with harty thankes geuen to god
becam a chylde agayne and sucked of the wysdome which cometh from
aboue & saueth all that be noryshed therwith in the which he contynued to
his lyfes ende with the honour and glorye to God to whome be prayse for
euer.[39]

For the four years he had left, Rastell devoted himself to the cause of the
new religion. Increasingly separated from More, he was gradually drawn
into a relationship with Cromwell. Some Statute printing was thrown his
way, in connection with a new and slightly improved edition of his Statutes *Abridgement*, which was printed by William Rastell and perhaps
even edited by him rather than his father.

Immediately after his conversion there was a plan to make Rastell
master of Christ Church, a secularized priory in Aldgate, which came to
nothing, and a plan to establish him and Martin Pyrry in an office supervising legal instruments in the City of London, which probably did come
to fruition. He and Cromwell and others got mining rights on Dartmoor,
and in 1534 he was considered well enough situated with the secretary to
be tentatively offered a bribe for influence to be exerted on the bishop of
Exeter to grant a farm to one John Arundell. None of this seems to have
brought any significant financial return at a time when Rastell's obses-
sion with reforming Church and State was leading him to disastrous
neglect of his legal and printing businesses. In 1534 the lawsuit between
him and the Skipwith family over his land lease in Hadley was settled in
their favour, and he lost his country house. Cromwell attached him to
Roland Lee, the new bishop of Coventry and Lichfield, for a commission
on law and order in Wales, and in at least one letter Lee urged strongly
that something should be done for this now aged enthusiast, who was too
honest to ask anything for himself.[40] But no help was forthcoming,
except for a few minor tasks for which he was just as likely not paid. The
one book surviving from the last years is only a prognostication and not
likely to have returned much of a profit.

The shop at the Mermaid, as Rastell would complain to Cromwell, had
declined very badly. From 1532 it seems to have been left entirely in the
hands of an apprentice, William Mayhewe, who was only twenty when
he made his disposition in Chancery in 1535, and from at the latest 1534
half the shop was left in control of the Protestant bookseller John Gough,
who was said to have had much more of the house available to him than
previous tenants, despite Mayhewe's efforts to keep a full half of the
shop for Rastell's purposes.[41] In a series of letters to Cromwell, almost
certainly in 1534, Rastell indicated that his press had suffered along with
his printing business and hoped that his zeal for the new religion would

be matched by the vicegerent himself, who had patronage and money to bestow.[42] His first plan was for a book called "The Book of the Charge," which would establish true religion through being read at courts and assizes, "whereby not only the lernyd men them selff*es* but also the people shalbe instructyd in true lernyng & brought from ignorauns to knolege of the true feyth & to haue no co*n*fidence in *the* pope." He had involved Sir Francis Bigod in this work as well; ironically, both were to lose their lives in what they considered the service of their volatile king.

Another letter indicates that the book was sent back to him for alterations, either by Cromwell himself or by the Council, and for the first time raises Rastell's financial troubles. His one experiment with the English people's willingness to pay for their Reformation, the printing of the Primer that he had compiled, was evidently a failure, and almost the final blow to a printing house that for three years had been devoted to reform tracts that Rastell himself admitted were unsaleable. It is a lengthy letter that not only deals with the problem of disseminating the doctrines of the English Reformation, but also raises Rastell's last hope for financial security through official or Crown subsidy of the printing of books. It needs to be quoted in full:

> Pleasith it yo*ur* maystership to understand *tha*t as touchyng my bok*e* which ye delyu*e*rd me to be refomyd I must besech you to gyff me a lityll leyser for this .x or xij days, for the matter is weyghty & requireth good lernyng wherfore I *pur*pose to corober it w*ith* mo auctoryties & to add many mo thyng*es ther*to, that when I shall bryng it to you agayn it shall be a n*other* man*er* boke than it was, Also I must desyre you of two petycions, One is when ye shall shew it to king*es grac*ce or to *other* of hys counsell yf ther shalbe found any dowt*es therin tha*t I may be hard to replye *ther*to satisfye such argume*nt*es & reasons as shalbe alegyd to the contrary, My second petycion is that as I haue takyn payn in *the* drawynge *ther*of that I may be made p*r*euey to the p*er*fityng *ther*of when it shalbe set forth by the auctorite of the kyng*es* commyssyon, ffor yf it may be brutyd that it com-myth of the kyng*es* mynd & that hys g*r*ace hath studyed the matt*er* I trust it wyll do as grete good as any lytyll boke that hath bene yet put abrode And when it shalbe so put in execution mee thynkith it wold do verey well that there shuld be x or xij m of those bok*es* of this charge printyd and gy-ffyn in to eu*er*y shyre of englond sparklyd abrode among the people which may be done vnder the cost of C li., Also I must besech you to be *con*tent that I may moue you now of a n*other* matt*er* touchyng my selff, yt is not unknowen vnto you *tha*t I haue spend my tyme & gyffyn my bysynes p*r*in-cipally this iiij or v yer*es* in co*m*pylying dyu*er*s bok*es* conc*er*nyng the fortherauns of the kyng*es* causis & opposi*n*g of the pop*es* vsurpyd auc-torite & therby gretly hyndered myn own bysynes that as I shall answer

afore god I am the wors for it by a C li & aboue, and beside that I haue de-
cayd the trade of my lyffyng ffor where before that I gate by the law in ple-
dyng in westminster hall xl mark a yere that was xx nobles a terme at the
lest and printyd euery yere ij or iij C reame of papyr which was more yere-
ly profet to me than the gaynys that I gate by the law, I assure you I get not
now xl s a yere by the law nor I prentyd not a C reame of papyr this ij yere,
therfore syr yf it please you to consider. I haue longyd & leyned vnto your
maystership specyally before any other of the kynges counsell thys iiij or
v yeres and though I haue not done vnto you so good seruyce & pleasure
as other men haue done, yet I haue done it wyth as good a mynd & wyll as
some other which make more of them selffes than I do. And I purpose yet
styll to contynue my hert & good mynd vnto you with all the wit and power
that I haue, as long as I see that ye cleue to goddes causis & the kynges so
surely and truly as it apperith that ye do, Syr I am an old man I loke not to
lyff long and I regard ryches as mich as I do chyppes saue only to haue a
lyffyng to lyff out of det, and I care as mych for worldly honour as I care
for the fleyng of a fethyr in the wynd But I desyre most, so to spend my
tyme to do somewhat for the commyn welth as god be my Iuge wherfore
this I hertely now besech you, yf it please the kynges grace that this boke
of thys charge shalbe set forth or any part therof and also imprentyd ac-
cordyng as I before here haue shewd, that I may haue the prentyng therof,
it is but for a pennyworth work a peny for I shall peraduenture in the prentyng therof remember some poyntes to be amendid with councell which a
nother prenter that hath not studyed it shall not so sone fynd, Also yf it
lyke you I haue deuysid certeyn prayers to be put in primers of dyuers
sortes of small price which I did send to the court which be to bryng the
people which rede then from the beleue of the popes naughty doctrine, for
I do consyder that the most part of the people be loth to bye any such bokes
and yet yf they be gyffyn to them they wyll skantly rede them Therfor
when the matter in englyssh is put in primers which they vse to brynge
with them to the church they shalbe in a maner compellyd to rede them
Therfore yf the kynges grace wold do the cost to prent iiij or v M & gyff
them among the people which wold not cost aboue C li it wold turn the my-
ndes of the people & bryng them to the ryght beleue and do as mich good
as the prechynges do.

Though this desperate plea for help was obviously ignored, Rastell soon
wrote again to urge the licensing and distribution of "The Book of the
Charge" at the king's costs and to suggest more projects, including an
authorized book of sermons on every Gospel reading of the year "to be
prentyd & send vnto euery curate" to preach week by week, which could
have suggested the later *Book of Homilies*. In the same letter he also
makes suggestions for small books arguing that priests might marry and

work for a living, that images should not be venerated, and that the prayers of the living could not help the dead—two at least of these to be followed by bills in Parliament. This too was ignored.

In February 1535 the Proclamation on Tithes made it clear that the change in religion would by no means change the ways in which religion was financed.[43] Rastell seems to have put himself well into the forefront of opposition, arguing at some kind of public meeting in London that tithes were against the laws of nature, of man, and of God.[44] It was not an argument likely to have much effect on Archbishop Cranmer and Bishop Gardiner of Winchester, who agreed, for once in their lives, on this approach to church finance. Gardiner affected not to understand what Rastell meant by the laws of nature, man, and God, but insisted that in the order of nature the lowest creatures worked hardest and the highest least and that, therefore, Rastell's argument that tithes were an intolerable burden to the poor and merely kept the rich from doing works of charity could be ignored. For the law of man, he added, the king's taxes were not based on "gaynes or losses" but weighed equally on the successful merchant and the one "that loseth in his conuey." "To which reasons," Harcoke added, "*master* Rastel made no answer but sung agayne his olde song, of which the Archbishop of caunterburie was werye and said if he had any new reasons they shuld be hard, but as for the old they be sufficientlye digested."[45]

Whether because of the tithes dispute or because Rastell was a debtor to the king, or because he had gone too far in propagating the Reformation, he was soon imprisoned and held without trial until his death. In one last letter he appealed to Cromwell for help:

> Now at the last my good lord haue some Remembraunces of me a pore prisoner, bywrapped w*ith* care thought & heuynes, p*er*turbyd w*ith* languor sorrow & pensyfenes, oppressyd w*ith* extreme poue*r*tye, And now by long imp*re*sonment brought to extreme mysery, for saken of my ki*n*smen, destytute of my frendys, aydlesse confortlesse and sucourlesse I am now non other but euyn obprobrium et abiectio plebis, this crosse of adue*r*syte hath god layd vppon my nek which I will not grudge to bere ffor Chrystes sake to whom I and all men ar synners & offenders Neuertheless yet I am very sure of my self that I haue not so offendyd the kyng*es* highnes no nor comyttyd any thyng agaynst the lawes of the Realm wherin I haue Iustly dese*r*uyd this long ponyshme*n*t that I haue sustaynyd If I myght come to answer I wold lyttyll dowt but that I could sure excuse me to the shame and confusyon of my malycouse accusers. If I durst be so bold to say it me thynk I haue grete wrong this long season to haue byn kept in dura*n*s w*ith*owt comyng to any answere If the kyng nor his counsell be not at leisure to here the cause yet at the lest me thynk the Cryme is not such but that I

myght well haue my pore carcas at lyberte fyndyng suertye to be forth comyng to answere to all thynge*s* that shall or may be obiected agaynst me.[46]

Such a request was only for the justice and equity guaranteed by the laws of the realm, he added; nor should he be kept in prison penniless, to live on "almys and charyte." Only Cromwell could help him, especially if his imprisonment was at the king's own order.

On 25 June 1536 John Rastell was dead. It is not known whether he died alone or with his family about him. Nor is it known where he was buried. That he died impoverished, imprisoned, and slightly regarded by his newer associates without leaving a clear statement of why he was in jail and without coming to trial can only be seen as sadly ironic for someone whose cause and device had been "Iusticia Regat": his ambition had always been to serve the commonwealth of England, he had continually hoped that his services would bring him modest fame and modest wealth, and he had devoted all his energies to advancing and promulgating the causes of reason.

Notes

1   John Rastell, *Pastime of People,* (entry 47 below), [2]E6.

2   Public Record Office, State Papers, SP1/113/2179; abstracted in *L&P,* 11, 1487.

3   Rastell's will, Prerogative Court of Canterbury, PCC 3 Crumwell.

4   A.W. Reed, *Early Tudor Drama* (London, 1926). This account of Rastell's early life has endured very well; neither later scholarship nor my re-examination of Reed's sources has added much to that great work. Further, Reed's devotion to Rastell was matched only by his skill with the public records. The only document used in this study that was not known to Reed is the post-mortem inventory of his stock, for which see R.J. Roberts, "John Rastell's Inventory of 1538," *The Library* 6th ser. 1 (1979), pp. 34-42.

5   For Rastell's life see also the accounts of Geritz and Laine in various places, which do not supersede Reed: Albert J. Geritz, *A Critical Edition of John Rastell's "The Pastyme of People" and "A New Book of Purgatory"*(New York, 1985), and "The Dramas and Prose Works of John Rastell," Ph.D. dissertation, University of Missouri at Columbia, 1976; Amos Lee Laine, "John Rastell: An Active Citizen of the English Commonwealth," Ph.D. dissertation, Duke University, 1972; and Albert J. Geritz and Amos Lee Laine, *John Rastell* (Boston, 1983).

6   *Victoria County History: Warwickshire,* 8 (1969), p. 479 refers to
     Thomas Rastell as "a lawyer, whose place of origin was unknown"
     when he became MP in 1472. Earlier, in 1443, a Thomas Rastell
     was warden, according to *The Coventry Leet Book,* ed. Mary Dor-
     mer Harris, Early English Text Society original series 134, 135,
     138, 146 (London, 1907-1913), p. 201. There are references to this
     Thomas, described as a "Deyster," at pp. 211, 247, 256, and 352.
     Isabel Rastell was taxed for soldiers to fight the Lancastrians in
     1461 and again in 1471. When Thomas became MP in 1472, a John
     Rastell became Warden of the Hospital of St. John Baptist, Coven-
     try (*VCH Warwickshire,* 3 (1908), p. 111). All this suggests that the
     family were of fairly long standing in Coventry; presumably they
     had ties, business or family, in London. They were probably related
     also to the Rastells in Gloucestershire. Thomas was the father of the
     John Rastell this study concerns.

7   *Records of Early English Drama: Coventry,* ed. R.W. Ingram (Tor-
     onto, 1981) lists payments for membership in the Corpus Christi
     Guild, "De Iohanne Rastell Filio Thome Rastell," in four instal-
     ments between 1491 and 1494, the second by "Iohanne Seman" and
     the fourth "per manus Maystres Semons" (pp. 75, 76, 78, and 81).
     These appear also in *The Coventry Leet Book,* and are cited by
     Reed, *Early Tudor Drama,* p. 1.

8   Anthony Wood, *Athenae Oxonienses* (London, 1691), p. 38.

9   Reed, *Early Tudor Drama,* p. 2, citing the Black Book of the Mid-
     dle Temple. This title was a distinction; see Nicholas Harpsfield in
     Lives of Saint Thomas More, ed. E.E. Reynolds (London, 1936), p.
     59: "Neither were utter barristers commonly made then but after
     many years' study." See also Albert J. Geritz, "The Marriage Date
     of John Rastell and Elizabeth More" *Moreana* 52 (1976), pp. 23-24.

10   Reed, *Early Tudor Drama,* pp. 2-5. See also *The Coventry Leet
     Book,* pp. 603-605, p. 619. Rastell was succeeded as coroner in
     1509 by John Butler (p. 624).

11   P.S. Allen, *Opus Epistolarum Erasmi* 1(Oxford, 1906), p. 450.

12   Elizabeth F. Rogers, *The Correspondence of Sir Thomas More*
     (Princeton, 1947), p. 9, letter 4, note.

13   William Dugdale, *Monasticon Anglicanum,* ed. John Caley, Henry
     Ellis, and Bulkeley Bandinel, 2 (London, 1819), pp. 299, 314; and
     *Landboc, sive Registram, Monasterii Beatae Virginis et Sancti
     Canhelmi de Winchelcumbe,* ed. David Royce, 2 (Exeter, 1903), pp.
     564-565.

14   Allen, *Opus Epistolarum Erasmi,* 4 (Oxford, 1922), pp. 162-163.

15   Reed, *Early Tudor Drama,* pp. 7-9.

16   Reed, *Early Tudor Drama,* p. 10; Rastell's legal action against the

Mores late in his life occurred in two Chancery cases, Public Record Office, Chancery C1/880/9 and C1/883/8. The problem of the lease at Monken Hadley led to another suit at the same time, Req. 2/6/202, settled against him (C66/642).

17   Thomas Rymer, *Foedera,* 3rd ed., 6 (The Hague, 1741), p. 131. 18 Req. 2/3/192, edited by Reed as an appendix in *Early Tudor Drama.*

18   Req. 2/3/192, edited by Reed in *Early Tudor Drama.*

19   These ideas about Rastell's intentions are based on the depositions in Court of Requests, Req. 2/3/192 and the text of the *Interlude* (entry 12 in the Bibliography).

20   John M. Headley, *The Complete Works of St. Thomas More, 5, Responsio ad Lutherum* (New Haven and London, 1969), esp. pp. 836-840 for Bercula's editorial work on this difficult text.

21   H.R. Plomer, "John Rastell and his Contemporaries," *Bibliographica* 2 (1896), p. 439, from William Bonham's deposition in C24/1/3765.

22   Reed, *Early Tudor Drama,* pp. 13-16.

23   Sidney Anglo, *Spectacle, Pageantry, and Early Tudor Policy* (Oxford, 1969), pp. 196-197.

24   Reed, *Early Tudor Drama,* pp. 16-17. Details of the stage, the materials used to build it, and the costume stock are in the depositions in the case between Rastell and the unpaid builder of the stage, Req. 2/8/14, fully transcribed by A.W. Pollard in *Fifteenth Century Poetry and Prose* (London, 1903), pp. 307-321.

25   Plomer, "John Rastell and His Contemporaries," p. 439. The apprenticeship of Kele and of Dab or Tab to Pynson is documented in Stanley H. Johnston Jr., "A Study of the Career and Literary Publications of Richard Pynson" Ph.D. dissertation, University of Western Ontario, 1977, pp. 530-531.

26   SP1/89/2885.

27   Reed, pp. 14-16, and lawsuit C1/560/51.

28   Reed, pp. 18-20. Anglo notes that the accounts of Sir Henry Guildford "show that though Rastell was active in the preparation of these revels, he was not concerned with the roofing—though this had been his concern at the Field of Cloth of Gold" (pp. 217-218). Reed felt that the cosmographical roof design must have been Rastell's.

29   Reed, p. 20.

30   SP1/56/11.

31   See my study of this material, "Thomas More and his Printers," in *A Festschrift for Edgar Ronald Seary: Essays in English Language and Literature presented by colleagues and former students,*

eds. A.A. Macdonald, P.A. O'Flaherty and G.M. Story (St. John's, 1975), pp. 40-57.

32   The *Supplication* is STC 10883; More's response is STC 18092-18093.

33   John Fisher, *Assertionis Lutheranae Confutatio* (Antwerp, 1523), discussed by E. Surtz, *The Works and Days of John Fisher* (Cambridge, Massachusetts, 1967), esp. p. 313 and p. 319, and Jean Rouschausse, *La Vie et L'Oeuvre de John Fisher* (Niewkoop, n.d.), pp. 161-175.

34   STC 11387, A4-A5.

35   Public Record Office, Req. 2/8/14.

36   STC 11385, A4^v-A5.

37   L.A. Schuster, R.C. Marius, J.P. Lusandi, and R.J. Schoeck, *The Complete Works of St. Thomas More,* vol. 8, *The Confutation of Tyndale's Answer* (New Haven and London, 1973), p. 35.

38   The main points of Rastell's second book on purgatory, of which no copy exists, can be more or less put together from Frith's point-by-point response in STC 11385.

39   STC 11385, A3^v-A4^v.

40   Reed, *Early Tudor Drama,* pp. 22-23. The bill for Rastell to be made Master of Christ Church is in E36/143; the supervisory post is in Public Record Office, Exchequer, E36/139; the request for the Cornish mining interest is in SP2/ fol. 0 and the agreement in E41/219. The offer from Arundell is in SP1/85, abstracted in *L&P,* 7: 955. Lee's letter is also in SP1/85, abstracted in *L&P,* 7: 1151. The decision in favour of the Skipwiths as cited above is C66/642.

41   All this information and most of the information in the following "Typographical Preface" can be found in the Chancery suit studied by Plomer.

42   These letters as cited in the following pages can be found as SP1/85/5796, a following letter with the same number, and a third letter SP1/85/2885; abstracted in *L&P,* 7: 1071, 1073. Rastell's reputation as a writer for the Reformation was strong enough later for the Pilgrimage of Grace to include him with William Tyndale, Robert Barnes, William Marshall, and Christopher Saint Germain as heretics whose writings had to be suppressed: *L&P,* 6: 1246, 1250.

43   *Tudor Royal Proclamations,* ed. P.L. Hughes and J.F. Larkin, 1 (New Haven and London, 1964), no. 153. The proclamation does threaten imprisonment and fines for non-payment.

44   A Dr Harcoke who was also present at the meeting reported it in a written sermon.

45   SP6/9/2179, abstracted in *L&P,* 10: 2179.

46   SP1/113/2179, abstracted in *L&P*, 11: 1487.

TYPOGRAPHICAL PREFACE

In the will he made on 20 April 1536 Rastell left his wife "her Ioynter of my hous in saynt Martyns made to her by indenture *with* my presse not*es* and *lett*res comprised in the same and half my houshold stuf," and left some bequests to be paid from the sale of his stock of books.[1] Two years later his books were inventoried for his son William, administrator of the estate, by the King's Printer, Thomas Berthelet, and by William Bonham and Henry Dab, both printers who had worked with Rastell and knew him well. The house contained stocks both large and small of some 22 titles published there, and of about 49 other books either kept for sale or as Rastell's own library. The largest of the stocks was 787 copies of the *Primer* that Rastell had hoped to use royal sanction to impose on the English Church.

Remarkably absent, as R.J. Roberts noted in editing the inventory, are "the books that one would expect a practising lawyer to own"[2] or anything greatly suggesting the books forwarding the Reformation that Rastell claimed he had devoted the last four or five years of his life to writing. The books he wrote defending the pope's authority are also missing; it seems possible that Rastell himself got rid of these and, as Roberts suggests, William Rastell might have got rid of the others, destroying the Protestant books and absorbing the law texts for his own use.

Practically none of the inventoried books is of a late date, that is, after 1530, which tends to confirm Rastell's complaint to Cromwell in the year before his death that his zeal for the Reformation had cost him dearly:

> ... where before *tha*t I gate by *th*e law in pledyng in westm*inster* hall xl mark a yere that was xx nobles a terme at the lest and p*r*intyd eu*er*y yere ij or iij C reame of papyr which was more yerely p*r*ofet to me than *th*e gaynys *tha*t I gate by the law, I assure you I get not now xl s a yere by *th*e law nor I p*r*entyd not a C reame of papyr this ij yere.[3]

Indeed there was only one full-time employee in those years, though two journeymen appeared from time to time to do printing for Rastell on the one press the shop had, and half the shop and printing house were rented to John Gough, probably the most active distributor of Protestant books in all England.[4]

There is no evidence that Rastell himself ever worked at frame or press, something his standing as a gentleman and as a barrister would probably have prevented him from doing, and much to indicate that the writing and editing of books were his main concerns, since some three-quarters of the books he produced were his own work or that of other members of the More circle. His publications show sequential changes in style and appearance, suggesting that the actual printing—perhaps after some discussion—was left in the hands of one workman most of the time, with help as required from occasional hired journeymen. In the busiest period of his printing career, between 1525 and 1529, he is said to have withdrawn to his country house in Finsbury, where he "ther sometyme taried a quarter of a yere" while "the dores were shutt vp" at the house.[5]

From 1519 onwards he had a series of stationers as sub-tenants, with living quarters and the use of half the shop. While the printing house and the casting house were reserved for Rastell alone, or were until Gough's tenancy, the fact that they were stationers themselves implies some kind of profit-sharing agreement or an arrangement under which they could use the shop to sell books or other paper supplies while supervising or actually doing the printing. Changes in style are very marked at Rastell's press, and such changes do seem to coincide with changes of address or of sub-tenants. Fashions in book design and what readers might expect a current book to look like of course alter from time to time, and any number of workmen could imitate a modish typographic style, but every printer must make final choices about the layout of display material, the use of ornament, and matters such as line length and spacing in relation to page size. In making these decisions a printer leaves a sort of signature on a book or group of books. A modern printing house would have one or more designers and usually some kind of house style in appearance as well as spelling or punctuation; in the sixteenth century the senior workmen, with or often without discussion with the master, would certainly make such decisions. That there were changes in workmen as well as changes in the emphasis of Rastell's choice of publications is certain enough, as is the fact that his books can be seen to appear in five distinct and sequential styles, all of which can be dated and some of which can be seen as coinciding with the arrival of specific journeymen at his house.

1. 1509-1511 or 1512 (entries 1-2)

No firm date can be given for the establishment of his first printing house at "flete brydge at the abbot of wynchecombe his place," but it was probably in 1509, when he resigned as coroner of Coventry to move to London during the period when the accession of Henry VIII inspired such high hopes among humanists that Erasmus himself came to England from the great printing establishment of Aldus Manutius in Venice, which had been a centre for the much-travelled writer. Possibly Rastell was able to establish his press there with the support or encouragement of the abbot himself, the humanist Richard of Kidderminster; certainly he had the encouragement of Thomas More, whose translation of the life of Pico della Mirandola by Pico's nephew was Rastell's first publication. A fragment from an edition of John Stanbridge's *Long Accidence,* bound by accident in with a Wynkyn de Worde *Donatus* of about 1509, can be assumed to have belonged to the same period. Both books are quartos in sixes with thirty-one lines of text to a page, both in the type he used throughout his career, Isaac's 93a textura; both are neatly imposed, attractive books. The title of the Pico is an emphatic block of type, drawing the reader's eye by its solidity and its justified right margin. Lombardic capitals are used for openings in both books.

The 93a textura was clearly French; Isaac identified it as a variant of the 93 textura of Wolfgang Hopyl, a Parisian printer who did much work for the English stationers up to 1521; Rastell's type has a slightly different s (Isaac's s^2), a different-sized paragraph mark, a double hyphen, and no capital W. Another variant with a different s and w was acquired by Peter Treveris in 1522, and used by him to print or, sometimes, print part of books under Rastell's imprint. The types are most easily distinguished by the capital T, which has a diamond flourish within in Rastell's 93a textura but none in Treveris's 93b.

Since Rastell's last apprentice, William Mayhewe, referred in about 1535 to a "castynghowse" distinct from the printing house in Rastell's establishment, it can be assumed that Rastell owned the matrices and possibly the punches of the 93a textura, which he used throughout his entire printing career, and possibly those of the other faces he added as his business grew.

2. 1511 or 1512-1517 (entries 3-10)

After a year or two the press was moved to a shop at the south side of St Paul's Cathedral, beside Paul's Chain. Eight further books are known to have been printed there: four quartos in sixes, one small octavo, and three large folio law texts. Founts of 84 and 94 bastard type were bought for the production of law books, along with 116 textura for use in headings. Fifteen all-purpose ornamental strips that could be used for emphasis or to frame a title or colophon were acquired as well; they are obviously not new. And two printers' devices were done for the expanded shop, a small one with a criblé ground and the more elaborate large one. Both play on Rastell's initials and the motto "Iusticia Regat." The earlier device is McKerrow 40, in its earliest known appearance in the *Liber Assisarum* (late 1513 or 1514), but already showing signs of wear and nicks suggestive of earlier use in books no longer extant. It is a simple criblé rectangle centred on a shield with the monogram IR, John Rastell, and a ribbon with the initials expanded to "Iusticia Regat." Its borders were weak from the beginning, and a fault in planing the block gave it a tendency to faintness along its lower border, especially when it was printed close to anything else. Obviously it was intended to advertise Rastell's connection with the law.

The second device, in perfect condition in the *Liber Assisarum,* is McKerrow 37, a much more elaborate cut. Like McKerrrow 40, it very likely appeared in earlier books that have not survived. In fact the feathers of the Prince of Wales that appear in the upper right corner seem almost to suggest that the block was cut and used before the accession of Henry VIII in April 1509. But there is no other evidence to support this speculation, and certainly no reason to argue that Rastell was printing before the death of Henry VII. Given his concern for law and continuity, it is more likely that he designed the block to have the Royal Arms in the left and the feathers in the right to suggest the continuity of English law under primogeniture, even should there be no Prince of Wales at the actual moment. Between the shields is the Father of Heaven, surrounded by stars, with his hand raised in blessing; there are clouds beneath the two scrolls, the upper one elongated and containing the word of creation, "Fiat," and the lower rectangular with the monogram IR, signifying, as in the smaller device, both John Rastell and "Iusticia Regat." To the left is a merman flanked by planets and to the right a mermaid flanked by stars, with beams of grace descending on both from the Father above; the mermaid combs her hair with her left hand, and beneath them is a hemisphere of the globe, comprising the four elements of fire, air, water, and earth. Below all this, with its clear implications of Rastell's concern for cosmography and natural law, is another scroll with his name in full. The "Father of Heaven" device had no tendency to weak impressions and lasted through to the end of Rastell's printing career, with some breaks appearing in the mid-1520s.

Design, and line length in relation to page size in all these books, shows a similarity to the choices made in the Winchecombe Place books. There is a sparing use of ornament for emphasis, except in the octavo *Donatus Devotionis*, which is rather cluttered. There is further use of diminishing or expanding lengths of lines centred on themselves to create pyramid patterns that, combined with the openness of the spacing both between and within lines, resembles the style later to be characteristic of Thomas Berthelet's press at the Lucrece. The books look as if there was one man in complete charge of the press, and one could speculate that it was the printer Thomas Bercula, who later accompanied Rastell on his frustrated New World voyage of 1517, and even later acted as editor of Latin texts for Richard Pynson, the King's Printer. Whether Bercula and Berthelet—cultivated and humanist printers with friends within the More circle and similar printing habits—were one and the same man or not seems impossible to know.

By this time it is clear that Rastell's printing enterprise was very much an extension of the humanist ideals that More and others hoped to see dominating the court of Henry VIII. Its choice of texts and procedures reflected utopian ideals of education, religion and the simplification of law, as well as making use of the printing press, an invention that More's imagined utopians saw as the only useful thing Europe had to offer.

The printing business was also extended by a loose share agreement with Pynson and de Worde for the publication of the large law texts. The first of these, the *Liber Assisarum*, was done by Rastell's own press in 1513 to 1514, the date being indicated by its list of circuit judges for 5 Henry VIII, which ended 21 April 1514. In the preface, which, like the list, would have been printed after the text, Rastell wrote that he and "dyuers other gentylmen" had worked on the ordering of the book and "the imprinting of the same" and intended "further to put in print a nother boke which by goddis grace shall be beter done," this being the *Grand Abridgment* of Sir Anthony Fitzherbert, who was both a very learned lawyer and a friend of Rastell's from Coventry. Rastell's own press did the first of the three very large volumes, and had a little trouble in casting off the copy, which led to a few pages patterned to fill the paper page and to a couple of blanks. The two remaining volumes seem to have been printed by de Worde, whose 95 textura appears consistently, though the use of woodcuts from Pynson's stock shows that the King's Printer was one of the consortium. The books were complete on 21 December 1516 and sold at the considerable price of forty shillings. Rastell's *Tabula* to the *Abridgment* appeared on 10 February 1517, not long before his departure for the New World.

Among the humanist works printed were Henry Medwall's interlude *Fulgens and Lucrece* and Thomas Linacre's *Progymnasata*, which demonstrate further connections with the More circle. In design, both were virtually identical to the Pico book.

3. 1519-1520 (entries 11-12)

When Rastell returned to London, presumably in 1519, from what seems to have been an extended stay in Ireland, he had two important texts to get into print but no printing establishment. It was probably through his old associate Pynson that he got in touch with William Bonham, then twenty-two years old and doubtless fairly recently out of his apprenticeship, who found and negotiated a lease for him on the house in Cheapside at Paul's Gate that was later given the sign of the Mermaid. Why a young journeyman should negotiate a lease for a lawyer in the Middle Temple who had been an "utter barrister" since 1502 seems a mystery to me, but a lease with the Bridge House Masters began at Michaelmas 1519, and the first book was issued without an address a few weeks later, on 25 October.

This first book was a translation into English of statutes with penalties, apparently the first work of its kind, to some extent intended for educated laymen as well as for lawyers. It was as well Rastell's first publication of a work written by himself and was fairly soon followed by a second book of his own writing, the dramatic interlude of the *Four Elements*. Both books combined two of Rastell's greatest concerns—the moral as well as economic advantages to be derived from careful study and the importance of using the vernacular, which would both augment and improve the English language itself and also assert the dignity of the nation. Both themes were to inform the rest of his career.

The two books are octavos with their display type, an explicit in the abridgment and a title in the interlude, laid out simply and gracelessly as paragraphs, not centred on themselves but getting their emphasis from the use of paragraph marks and 116 textura for first lines. The texts are in the usual 93a textura, each with twenty-nine lines to a page, unattractively narrow margins, and more than a few uncorrected errors, including a faulty imposition in the *Statutes*. Their closeness in time is self-evident and supported by the fact that the unique copies in which they have survived were once bound together.

Clearly whoever was running the press for this brief period had little sense of book design and even seems incompetent; Rastell's apology for faults from his own pen "or elis by neclygens of the prynters" can be seen as more than a conventional prefatory disclaimer.

The advance made by the shop during this time was the casting of music type for single-impression printing, which had never been done before in England or on the Continent. Rastell and his workmen struck punches of stave lengths and notes into new matrices so they could cast an entire fount of music types. These were important enough to Rastell to be specified in his will, and are discussed further below.

The large printer's device appears in the 1519 *Statutes* showing for the first time a weakness in the left thumb of the Creator.

4. 1521-1527 or 1528 (entries 13-43)

About a year or so after the move to the house in Cheapside, Bonham became Rastell's sub-tenant with living quarters and the use of half the shop. He stayed for two years. While the press establishment—"the pryntynghowse the castyng howse & the garrett"—was reserved to Rastell along with half the shop, it seems possible or even probable that Bonham either did or supervised the printing in the house.

Whether this is correct or not, it is certain that somebody drastically changed the appearance of Rastell's books in 1520 or 1521. The usual format became small folio, with forty to forty-four lines to a page and line lengths in the vicinity of 130 millimetres. All the books were marked by an extensive use of ornament, with the decorative strips from the earlier law volumes made into frames around titles much of the time. Normally the larger printer's device (McKerrow 37) was used for emphasis, with two series of woodcuts, 23x23 and 23x14. Privileges appeared in all books after 1520, as was normal in the trade. The address used was Cheapside at Paul's Gate.

After two years Bonham moved on, presumably not to open his own business, since no book with his imprint occurs before 1542, but to other concerns or employment in the stationers' trade. His place was taken by "one Iohn Heron habberdasher which occupied the craft of Stacioner," who stayed for three years during which time little or nothing seems to have been printed. He was followed in 1524 or 1525 by Thomas Kele, a skilled printer who had been apprentice and journeyman with Pynson—as I think, though without proof, Bonham had been as well. His arrival coincided, it would seem, with Rastell's return from the country, where he had evidently been in the habit of staying for extended periods of time. Rastell appears to have brought with him a great deal of material for publication, works both legal and humanist. Kele stayed for about a year, after which Bonham returned for an unspecified period of time. Henry Dab or Tab, another man from the King's Printer's house, might have become associated as well between 1524 and 1528; he was later to act with Berthelet and Bonham in valuing Rastell's stock. Laurence Andrewe, a translator and editor like Rastell, who tried to start publishing with equipment borrowed from him, could have joined in too; he worked also with Peter Treveris of Southwark, who began printing some of Rastell's books for him at this time and seems likely to have been a relative of the Leonard Andrewe who did occasional printing for Rastell in the last years of his career.

The second half of this decade, then, was the busiest time Rastell's press would ever have, with his own books and books by other members of More's group of friends appearing regularly, in a more or less uniform format and style. Between 1524 and 1528, in fact, the books communicate a sort of exuberance by their appearance, signifying both the interests of a cultivated and fairly affluent humanist and the skills of a group of well-trained printers.

In 1525 the house was for the first time given the name, and no doubt also the sign, of the Mermaid, presumably because of the mermaid and merman theme in the large printer's device. From that year on the Mermaid address was used for most books, and some imprints were given playful forms of the legal formula *fieri facias*. The device itself suffered damage in 1525 with a break or weakening of the lower border appearing, sometimes as a clean break and sometimes partly inked in.

5. 1528-1532 (entries 44-52)

At some time between 1527 and 1529 another reorganization of the press occurred, following a change in Rastell's concerns. The seriousness of the Reformation crisis was becoming all too evident, along with the need for thoughtful and informed argument. The need to use English as the means of persuasion was clear, both to More, who was licensed to read heretical books for refutation, and of course to Rastell, who for at least ten years had been asserting the importance of the English language. The books reflect the gravity of their topics in their design: there is much less use of ornament; after some intermediary books in a plainer style there is a consistent use of the large or full-sized folio as a format; books have running titles, foliation, and catchwords, which had not been house practice before; and, as in earlier books, there is a tendency to create patterns in display matter by centring lines on themselves.

The last ornamented book was the full-size folio history the *Pastime of People*, the last book that could be called a product of Rastell's mature thought in leisure. It followed two plain and workmanlike octavos, a trilingual statute abridgment, and Christopher Saint Germain's *Doctor and Student*, and it is likely that its progress through the press was interrupted by the printing of More's *Dialogue of Heresies*. After the *Pastime*, Rastell himself entered the Reformation dispute with two successive printings of his *A new boke of purgatory*.

Whether or not there was a new workman in charge, there was obviously some reorganization of the printing house, at least partly intended to suggest authority and seriousness through the appearance of the books being printed.

The larger printer's device was repaired.

6. 1532-1536 (entries 53-59)

At some point in 1532 Rastell, while trying to convince the young reformer John Frith of the existence of Purgatory, suddenly converted to the reformers and, characteristically, decided to use his press entirely in the service of the new religion. His shop seems immediately to have begun a decline, to the point where only a young stationer, William Mayhewe, remained in charge. Mayhewe came to Rastell's service in 1532 when he was only seventeen, presumably as an apprentice stationer. His deposition in Chancery in 1535 asserts that he sold his master's books, but other "seruantes of the seid R" came from time to time to print. In other words, Mayhewe was not himself a printer. Half the shop was let to John Gough under terms which accord with the agreement Rastell had earlier had with Bonham and others. Gough was known very well in England as a distributor of Protestant books.

Gough was also not a printer, but like the others was able to hire them, and most certainly he used Rastell's music type for an edition of Myles Coverdale's *Goostly psalmes* (STC 5892). It seems possible that he could have overseen the printing—if it occurred—of the "dyuers bokes" against "the popes vsurped auctoryte" that Rastell claimed he had devoted the early 1530s to writing. It would seem that Gough's reforming activities gave him a special position in Rastell's esteem; Mayhewe implied in 1535 that keeping Gough out of the part of the house reserved to Rastell was difficult, and Bonham said directly that Gough was allowed more of the house than previous sub-tenants.

It seems impossible to know how many books were printed by Rastell's press or for him during these last three years. Much of the output could have been simply destroyed or lost through neglect. Rastell himself learned that "the most part of the people be loth to bye any such bokes and yet yf they be gyffyn to them they wyll skantly rede them." Rastell's last letters to Thomas Cromwell imply that during the last few years of its operation books from the Mermaid were, as he wrote of "the book of the charge" and his proposed other reforming books, fairly small; the term "lytyll boke" is normally used. But the books against the pope have not survived and are not inventoried with the other books in the shop, as mentioned above, and the only surviving book from the period is a prognostication, printed by Treveris, consisting of only one quarto gathering.

Whether the shop operated and sold books in the two years between Rastell's death and the inventory in 1538 is uncertain. Presumably his will was followed and the stock sold at that time. The printing stock was not inventoried; the types do not reappear at another press, and no more is known of the "dyuerse implementes belongyng ffor the craft of prynters" that Rastell's workmen had used so long to try to improve the world.

Notes

1   Public Record Office, Prerogative Court of Canterbury, PCC 3 Crumwell.
2   Roberts, p. 40.
3   Public Record Office, State Papers, SP1/85/2885, abstracted in *L&P,* 7: 1073.
4   Duff, pp. 58-59.
5   According to a deposition in Public Record Office, Chancery, C24/1/3765, a case studied by H.R. Plomer in "John Rastell and his Contemporaries," pp. 423-451. The depositions of William Bonham and William Mayhewe in this case give all the ensuing information about the sub-tenancies and staffing of Rastell's third printing house and its organization.

BOOK DESIGNS

Editor's Note: The examples given on the following pages are not always scanned to scale; those interested in relative size should consult the bibliographical descriptions in the third section of the book.

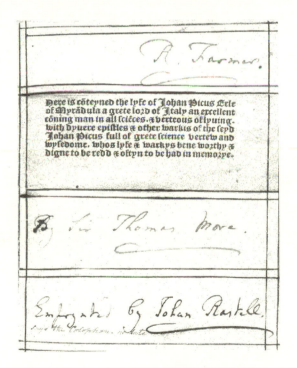

Design in first period, 1509-1511 or 1512: title page of More's *Life of Pico* (1); the rules are hand-drawn, and of a much later time.

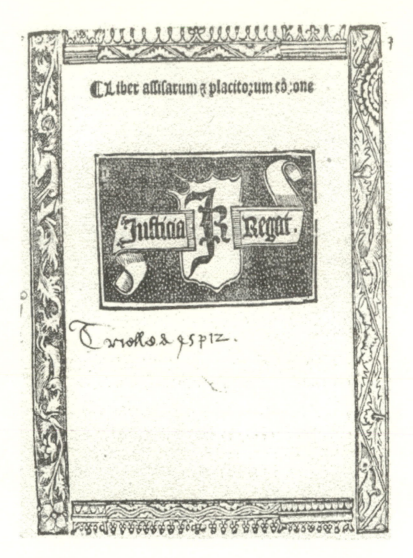

Design in second period, 1511 or 1512-1517: title page and explicit of the *Liber Assisarum* (3).

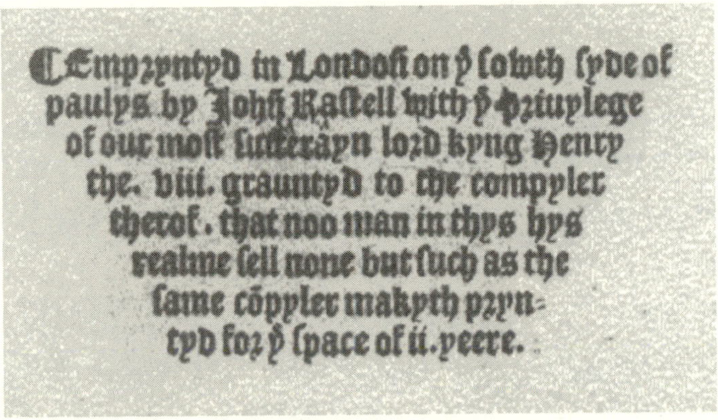

¶ Emprynted in London on ẏ sowth syde of
paulys by John Rastell with ẏ pryuylege
of our most souerayn lord kyng Henry
the. viii. grauntyd to the compyler
therof. that noo man in thys hys
realme sell none but such as the
same cõpyler makyth pryn-
tyd for ẏ space of ii. yeere.

Colophon from second period: Linacre's *Progymnasmata* (5).

¶ Adest finis p tēpore presenti
Thus ēdyth p abbreuiacōn of statutz trāslatyd
out of frēch ito ēglitsh by Johñ Rastell. & iprittd
by p same Johñ p xxb day of october in p xj pere
of p reyn of our souereyn lord kyng hēry the biij
wyth p prpuylege of our seyd souerei lord graū=
tyd to p seyd Johñ that no nother impzit agcyn
thys seid work   nor no nother ells where prin=
tyd of them sell wythin this realme duryng the
space of bij yersnext after this furst inpression.

Design in third period, 1519-1520: explicit with privilege from
Rastell's English *Abbreviation of Statutes* of 25 October 1519 (11).

¶A new iuterlude and a mery of the nature of the .iiij. elementꝭ declarynge many pro per poyntꝭ of phylosophy naturall/and of dyuers straunge landys/and of dyuers straunge effectꝭ & causis/whiche interlude yf ȳ hole matter be playde wyl conteyne the space of an hour and a halfe/but yf ye lyst ye may leue out muche of the sad mater as the messengers pte/and some of naturys parte and some of experyens pte & yet the matter wyl de pend conuenyently/and than it wyll not be past thre quarters of an hour of length.

¶Here folow the namys of the pleyers.

¶The messengere/Nature naturate/Humylyte Studyous desire/Sensuall appetyte/The tauer ner/Experyence/yngnoraunce/Also yf ye lyst ye may brynge in a dysgysynge.

¶Here folow dyuers matters whiche be in this interlude conteynyd.

¶Of the sytuacyon of the .iiij. elementꝭ that is to sey the perth the water the ayre and fyre/& of theyr qualytese and propertese/and of the generacyon & corrupcyon of thyngꝭ made of ȳ comyxton of them
                                             A.t.

Title page from third period: Rastell's *Interlude of the Four Elements* (12).

Design in fourth period: title page of Rastell's *Terms* of c. 1521 (14).

Title page from fourth period: Rastell's *Hundred Merry Tales* (15).

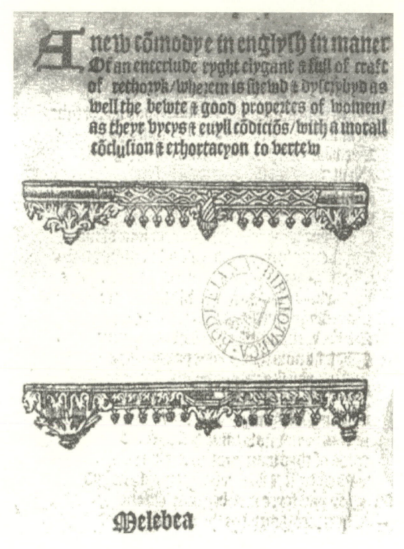

Title page from fourth period: *Calisto and Melebea* (22).

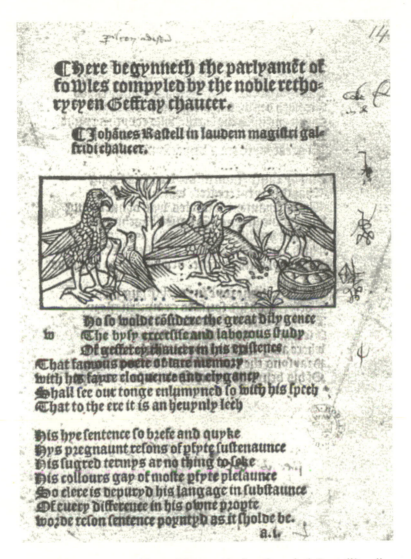

Opening from text without title page in fourth period: Rastell's edition of Chaucer's *Parliament of Fowls* (27).

Design from fifth period, 1528-1532; title page and colophon from Christopher Saint German's *Doctor and Student* (44).

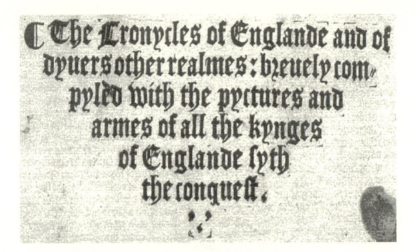

Title page from fifth period: letterpress title from Rastell's *Pastyme of People* (47).

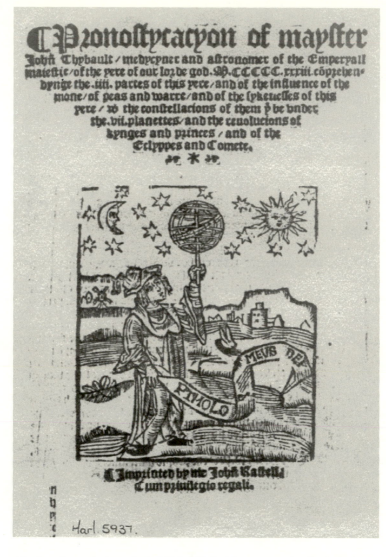

Design form sixth period, 1532-1536: title page and colophon from
Thibault's *Prognostication* (55).

Printer's Devices

Device McKerrow 40, a bordered criblé block, 27x89 mm., centered on a shield with Rastell's monogram and a scroll expanding the initials into the motto "Iusticia Regat." Its first known appearance was with the larger device McKerrow 37 in the *Liber Assisarum* of 1513-1514 (3). It was used infrequently, perhaps because it communicated only a concern for law, while the larger device included cosmographical concerns, or perhaps simply because it had weak borders and a tendency not to print clearly. Its last recorded appearance was in the anonymous *Life of St. Thomas a Becket*, which I have dated—not without reservations—at 1525-27 (28).

McKerrow 40 from the *Liber Assisarum* of 1513-1514 (3).

McKerrow 40 from Rastell's *Terms of the Law* of c. 1525 (14), with borders broken at left.

McKerrow 40 for "A wey mornynge" of c. 1525-1527 (25).

Device McKerrow 37, an historiated block, 103x72mm., suggesting Rastell's concerns and interests and the purposes for which he established his press. The top of the cut has centrally a depiction of the creating Word seen as Christ (John 1: 1-14), with the left hand held up palm outward and the right raised in blessing, with the first two fingers together and the other two folded. There are four stars on the right side and seven on the left, the seven perhaps reflecting Amos 5:8 and the total eleven Joseph's vision in Genesis 37:9. By the right hand the English Royal Arms appear, and by the left the feathers of the Prince of Wales, presumably intended to signify the continuity of law under primogeniture, and perhaps showing that the cut was made before 22 April 1509. On both sides light (Genesis 1:3) passes through clouds, while directly beneath a scroll bears the "Fiat" of creation.

Beneath all this, occupying the centre of the block, is a tableau with a male, scaly as a fish in his left leg, rising out of waters, his head surrounded by the sun and moon and what seems to be one planet, while to the right a corresponding female, scaly in the right leg, stands combing her hair, her head surrounded by what appear to be four other planets. Between them they hold a fringed cloth or veil containing Rastell's monogram; the woman merely holds it while the man is tearing it from its upper right corner. I assume it represents the veil of the Temple, rent at the moment of Christ's death (Luke 23:45) and that it implies the clear revelation of the Gospel by its being torn away.

A hemisphere beneath the central tableau represents the round earth, comprised of the four elements in ascending order of worth, from earth to fire. The male and female rise through these, as they are made of them, with their bodies from the waist down in the physical elements and from the waist up in the heavens, where they observe the planets and stars and tear the veil to achieve their vision of God.

The corresponding male and female doubtless represent completeness. The fish aspect of their appearance would seem to suggest both Mark 1:16-17, for they comprise the humanity the Apostles are there called upon to fish for, and also the early Church's use of the anagram and symbol of the fish as Christ, Son of God and Saviour, since He is both God and man born of woman.

From the top down the symbols represent the creating and ordering forces of law: the law of God enlightening the law of mankind and allowing it further enlightenment through the vision of the heavens and the tearing away of the veil before the Holy of the Holies, and the law of mankind remaining firmly rooted within the law of elemental nature. Wisdom and the reign of justice on earth could only come through an understanding of all three. Rastell's law-book prefaces and his *Interlude of the Four Elements* make this point very clear.

Finally, a scroll at the base contains Rastell's name.

McKerrow 37 from the *Liber Assisarum* of 1513-1514 (3).

McKerrow 37 from Rastell's *Abridgment of Statutes* of 25 October 1519 (11). Damage or a point of wear is evident in the thumb of the creating Word's left hand.

McKerrow 37 from Littleton's *Tenures* of c. 1525 (19) with a break in the lower border possibly caused by a sort crushing the border, and one in the top border.

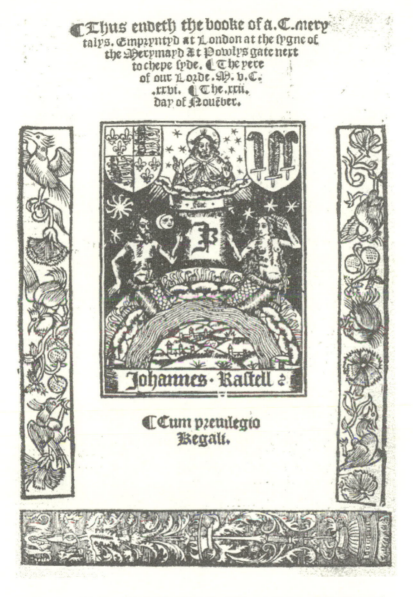

McKerrow 37 from Rastell's *Hundred Merry Tales* of 22 November 1526 (35) with the lower break slightly more evident, but the upper inked in.

McKerrow 37 from *Calisto and Melebea* of c. 1525-1527 (22), with the break totally clear.

McKerrow 37 from Christopher Saint Germain's *Doctor and Student* of 1528 (44). The device seems to have been repaired, probably by affixing reglet to the border after planing it, or possibly by steaming the breaks to bring the compacted wood up to height to paper, as printers did with crushed wood type until fairly recently. However, the weakness where the break in the base had occurred in about 1525 did recur practically at once. Beale's idea that the device was "recut about 1527, being a trifle wider and one eighth of an inch higher" is clearly wrong if he meant that the device had been recut as a new block; the weak spot in the left thumb of the creating Word shows it was indeed the same one.

Ornamental Strips

Ornamental strip 1, 9x73mm.

Ornamental strip 2, 9x94mm.

Ornamental strip 3, 9x94mm.

Ornamental strip 4, 9x94mm.

Ornamental strip 5, 11x134mm.

Ornamental strip 6, 11x132mm.

Ornamental strip 7, 11x134mm.

Ornamental strip 8, 11x134mm.

Ornamental strip 9, 11x134mm.

Ornamental strip 10, 13x94mm.

Ornamental strip 11, 13x92mm.

Ornamental strip 12, 14x88mm.

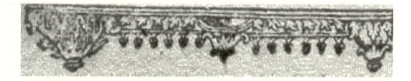

Ornamental strip 13, 14x92mm.

Ornamental strip 14, 19x139mm.

Ornamental strip 15, 22x115mm.

Other cuts occurring in Rastell books are the property of Peter Treveris.

Types

Rastell's types were described by F.S. Isaac in *English & Scottish Printing Types 1501-35*1508-41* (Oxford, 1930), figures 36-43. Isaac did his work very well, in my opinion, and I do not really see much to add to his account except the conclusions of A. Hyatt King about the music types, published as"The Significance of John Rastell in Early Music Printing," *The Library*, 5th ser. 26 (1972), pp. 197-214.

As noted above, Rastell's establishment included a casting house as well as a printing house, so he probably had matrixes if not punches for his types, especially the 93a textura he used through his whole career.

220 textura, with w^5 and s^3, first used in c.1524-1525 in *A Hundred Merry Tales* (15).

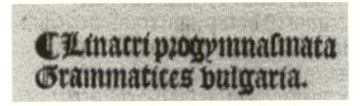

116 textura, with an s with top serif, v^3, w^2, and pointed h, used by Wynkyn de Worde and others, first used by Rastell in the title of the *Liber Assisarum* in 1513-1514 (3), here shown in title of Linacre's *Progymnasmata* of c.1514 (5).

93a textura, with s^2, v^3, w^{5a}, a diamond-centred capital T, large and small capital I, and no capital w, first used in More's *Life of Pico* in c.1509-1512, and then consistently in most of Rastell's books to 1536. Isaac identified it as a variant of the 93 textura of Wolfgang Hopyl, a Parisian printer who did much work for English stationers up to 1521. Another variant with a different s and w and plain capital T was acquired by Peter Treveris in 1522, and used to print whole books or sometimes part of books under Rastell's imprint. The founts are most easily distinguished by the capital T, which has a diamond flourish in Rastell's 93a, as mentioned above, but not in Treveris's 93b textura.

93a textura in More's *Life of Pico* in c.1509-1512 (1).

The boke of... new cardy
pleyeng at cardf one m...y lerne to know...
spel...e to rede...how one shuld wryte engl...
to rede all nöbers as well comī nöbers...
And also to lerne to cast accompt as...
countys as algozyfine wyth dyuers...
encys and cóclusyons as here after in...
specyally shalbe declaryd

What dyuers pper conceytf ād sciences folk...
lerne in pleyeng at yees cardys
Of y̆ order of yees cardf...e how yey shalbe...
be ye better parfcpuyd
How y̆at euery card beryth a dyuers letter...
mddys
For what cause the lettrs be set in the...
ye cardys
Off yees letters. y. and. w.

a.i

93a textura from *Book of the New Cards* of 1525-1527 (26), with Rastell's experimental letter *th* or, as Isaac calls it, "a y without a tail" occurring four times.

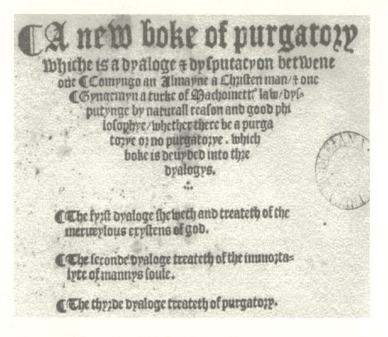

¶A new boke of purgatory
whiche is a dyaloge & dysputacyon betwene
one ¶Comyngo an Almayne a Chrysten man/& one
¶Gyngemyn a turke of Machomettʒ law/dys-
putynge by naturall reason and good phi
losophye/whether there be a purga
torye or no purgatorye . which
boke is deuyded into thre
dyalogys.

❧

¶The fyrst dyaloge sheweth and treateth of the
meruaylous exystens of god.

¶The seconde dyaloge treateth of the immorta-
lyte of mannys soule.

¶The thyrde dyaloge treateth of purgatory.

93a textura from Rastell's *New Book of Purgatory* of 10 October 1530 (48).

93b textura, with s^3, v^3, w^{5b}, and a plain capital T, but otherwise identical to Rastell's 93a textura. It was Peter Treveris's type, used by him in several books printed for Rastell, and in some books divided between the two shops, such as in *Hundred Merry Tales* of 22 November 1526 (35) or More's *Dialogue of Heresies* of June 1529 (46).

And syche I verply byleue
that yf he had bene gyltye
he neuer coud haue gotten
in such an bryghtnous mut
der eny pardon of the kyngys hyghnes/ I dare make
my selfe mych more bold of
his innocency now. For ye
shall vnderstad that he neuer sued pardon therfore.
But after longe examyna-
tyon of the mater/as well
the chauncellour as other/
beynge endyghted of the
dede & arrayned vppon the
entyghtement in the kyn-
gys bench/pledid that they
were not gyltie. And ther-
uppon the kyngys grace
beynge well & suffyeyently
enfourmyd of the trouthe / &
of hys blyssed dyspofycyon
not wyllig that there shold
in hys name eny false ma-
ter be maynteynyd/gaue in
comaundemet to hys attur-
ney to confesse theyr plees
to be trewe wythout any
farther troble. which thing
in so faythfull a prynce is
a clere declaracyon that the
mater layd to the chauncellour was vntrew.

54 textura, Treveris's type, found
only in the errata and paste-in in
More's *Dialogue of Heresies* in
June 1529 (46).

 vtlary   Fo.cc.lriiii

ſhall be warnyd to come & to maynteyn that the
wytnes is not trew which ſhalbe tryed and lyke
wyſe the kynges ſeruaūt and attorney ſhalbe re
cepyrd yf it be at the kynges ſewt.v'C.iii.c.riii.

C Loke moꝛe foꝛ vtlary in the tytles erigēt char
ter de pdon cheſtyꝛſhyꝛe and lancaſter.

S   J   R   J   S.

C Enpꝛynted in the chepeſyde at the ſyg
ne of the mere mayde nert to poulys ga=
te the.rrii.day of Deecber in the.rir
yere of the reyngne of oure ſo
uerayne loꝛde kinge Henry
the.viii.
C per me Johannem Raſtell
A D. MDXXVII.
Cum pꝛiuilegio. Regali.

67 rotunda, possibly Treveris's, as it is found in the *Abridgment of Statutes* of 22 December 1527 (43). It is also used for a series of standard small law texts in 1527- 28 (37-42).

94 bastard, which Isaac says has "various w's;"
like the rotunda, it was used in law books, first
as the text type for the *Liber Assisarum* of 1513-
1514 (3); shown here from *Tenures* of c.1524
(13).

84 bastard, first used in the *Tabula Libri Magni Abbreviamenti* of 10 February 1517 (10).

81 bastard, Treveris's type, used for the Law French text of Rastell's *Terms* of 15 July 1527 (36).

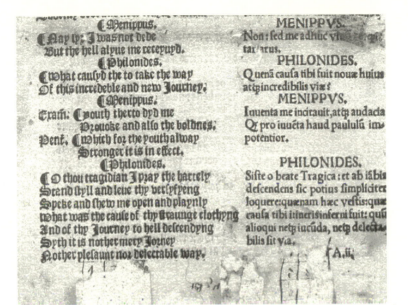

94 roman, Treveris's type used in only one Rastell book, Lucian's
Necromantia of c.1525-1526 (21).

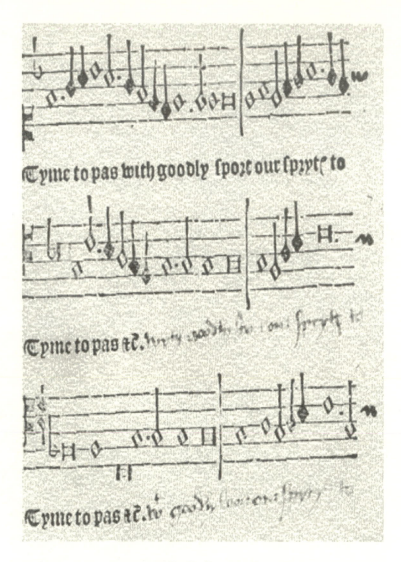

Music type or "notes," specifically listed in Rastell's will, and apparently the first music type cast for single-impression printing; see above and the notes to Bibliography 11.

Various Cuts

Woodcut on title page of Medwall's *Fulgens and Lucrece* (7).

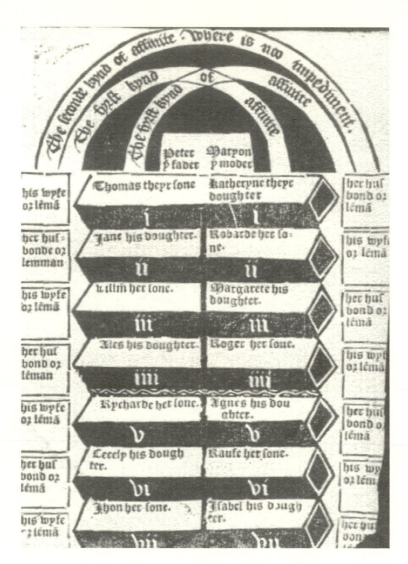

Table of affinity from the earlier edition of Harrington's *Commenda-tions of Matrimony* (8). Rastell's later edition has the table reduced to five places (9), but John Skot's reprint in 1528 gives all seven again (STC 12799 and 12800).

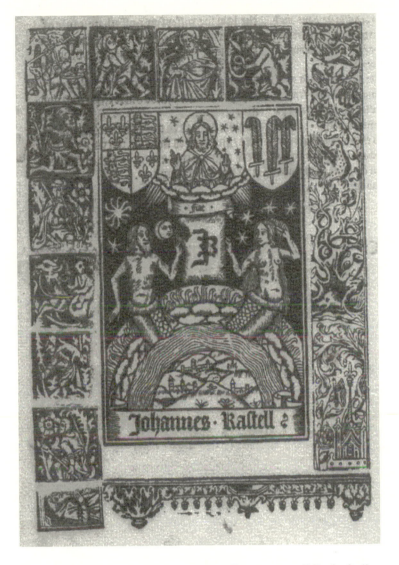

The frame around the device in Rastell's *Tenures* (13), including nine woodcuts from the 23x23 series and one from the 23x14 series.

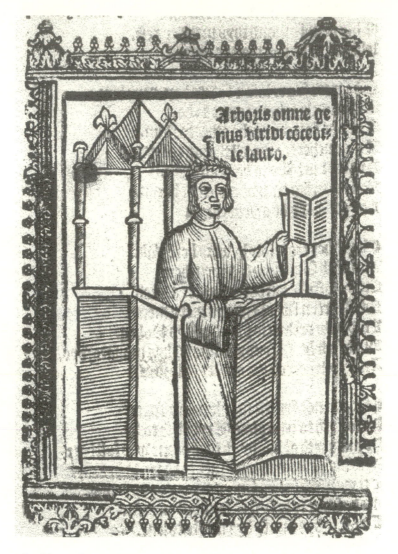

The illustration Hodnett 2287 on the title page of Skelton's *Against a comely Coystrowne* (29).

The arrangement of a page in the *Pastime of People* (47).

The Conqueror from the *Pastime of People* (47), with symbols of war, including the arrow that killed King Harold. The King's name appears above the woodcut; the following woodcuts were mortised to allow the headings to be set within.

Edward III as warrior, lawgiver, founder of the Order of the Garter, and King of England and France, from the *Pastime of People* (47).

Edward V, as uncrowned boy king, from the *Pastime of People* (47).

Bibliography

BIBLIOGRAPHY

1 *Life of Pico*

Giovanni Francesco Pico della Mirandola, . . . *lyfe of Iohan Picus*, translated by Thomas More, dedicated to Joyeuse Leigh in c.1505. c. 1509-12. 4° in sixes. Reprinted by Wynkyn de Worde c.1525 (STC 19898) and in *The Workes of Sir T. More,* edited by William Rastell, in 1557 (STC 18076).

Title: **Here is coteyned the lyfe of Iohan Picus Erle | of Myradula a grete lord of Italy an excellent | coning man in all ſcieces.& verteous of lyuing. | with dyuers epiſtles & other warkis of the ſeyd | Iohan Picus full of grete ſcience vertew and | wyſdome. whos lyfe & warkys bene worthy & | digne to be redd & oftyn to be had in memorye.**

Colophon: **Enprynted at london by Iohan Raſtell | dwellyng at yᵉ flete brydge at the abbot | of wynchecombe his place.**

Collation: 4°, A^2 a^4 b-f^6 g^4, 40 unnumbered leaves; $3 (-ae2, ag3) signed, A2 signed A [textura].

Contents: A1: title (verso blank). A2: **"Vnto his right entierly beloued ſiſter | in criſt Ioyeuce Leigh thomas more | gretyng in our lorde. | M**[lombardic cap^2] **It is** ..." to A2^V. al: **"The life of Iohn Picus | Erle of mirandula. | I** [text cap^8] **Iohan Picus** ...", text in 29 chapters each beginning lombardic cap^2, except on 64 and C1, text cap^3, to c3: **"Finis.".** c3^V: three epistles of Pico to el^V. On el^V: commentary on Psalm 15 (16), *Conserva me, Domine,* to e6^V. fl: Pico's twelve rules for spiritual battle to f5^V: Pico's twelve conditions of a lover to f6. On f6: ballad of the twelve properties to g3. On g3: prayer of Pico to g4^V. On g4^V: **"Amen."** | colophon.

Type: text (b3) 31 11., 145 (149) x 96, 93a textura.

Examined: British Library C.33.e.41.

Notes: STC 19897.7; Gibson 67; University Microfilms 122. More accurate dating seems not to be possible. Elizabeth Frances Rogers in *The Correspondence of Sir Thomas More* (Princeton, 1947) dates the translation at about 1505, basing the dating on Thomas Stapleton's *Tres Thomae*, in which the translation was connected with More's decision to live as a married Christian layman, taking Pico as his model. A missing word, Aeaea, on c3^v and the space left for it suggest that More did not see the book through the press.

2   *The long Accidence*

John Stanbridge, *The long Accidence*. c.1509-1512. 4° in sixes. Printed earlier and later by Wynkyn de Worde and others (STC 23153.4 in 1495 to 23154.3 in 1519).

Title, colophon, and most of text missing. The surviving fragment consists of b3.4, signed (textura). Sections begin with lombardic caps[2].

RT: **Accidence. | Accidence.**

Type: text (b3) 31 11., 145 (154) x 96, 93a textura.

Examined: John Rylands University Library of Manchester.

Notes: STC 23153.8 (Addenda 3) bound in sequence in $b of de Worde's *Donatus* of c.1508-1509 (STC 7016.4).

3   *Liber Assisarum*

Liber Assisarum et Placitorum Corone, edited, indexed, and prefaced by John Rastell. c. 1513-1514. 2°.

Title: within a frame of ornamental strips, left 8, upper 4, right 5, lower 2, 134x117 enclosing 116x95] **¶Liber aſſiſarum & placitorum corone** | [device McKerrow 40]

Explicit: **Aſſiſarum liber & plitorū corone foeliciſ explicit | Si iuuat anglorum reuerendas diſcere leges | Et cupis ex paruo diſcere multa libro | Chalcographi Raſtel ſtudioſos noſce labores | et librū aſſidue. plege. doctus eris**.

Collation: 2°, π^4 a-b^8 c-z^6 A- R^6 s^8 (-S8), 253 unnumbered leaves; $3 (-pl, +abS4) signed, missigning a4 (a3) [bastard].

RT: **Anno | primo** [to **quinquageſimo**].

Contents: π1: **"Tabula libri aſſiſarū & plitorum corone"** | [within a frame of ornamental strips, left 9, upper 2, right 5, lower 3, 171x115 enclosing 154x94, device McKerrow 37] | [device McKerrow 40]. $\pi1^v$: **"Prologus Iohīs raſtell in laudem legū** | T[lombardic cap]**horow ..."**, text to $\pi2^v$. π3: list of Circuit Judges for 5 Henry VIII (22 April 1513-21 April 1514). $\pi3^v$: **"Tabula plītorum corone"** | text in two columns to $\pi4^v$ al: title. a1^v: [explanation by Rastell of his indexing system and "the nombers of algorisme"]. a2: **"Aſſiſa Anno primo E. tercii** | 1. V[lombardic cap^2]**n aſſiſe ..."**, text arranged chronologically to S7^v, sections beginning with lombardic caps^2. On S7^v: explicit. S8 excised in copies seen and presumably blank.

Type: text (p4) 44 11., 205 (222) x 130 (160 to sidenotes and arabic numerals in inner margins), 94 bastard, openings of statements 93a textura, headings and running titles 116 textura.

Examined: British Library C.122.f.5; Cambridge Syn.4.51.7; Harvard Law Library Beale R48 (with explicit), Beale R49 (without explicit).

Notes: STC 9599; Beale R48, R49; Dibdin 843; University Microfilms 1171.

The inclusion of the list of Circuit Judges for 5 Henry VIII in the preliminaries, which were no doubt prefixed to the text after it had been printed, dates the book obviously enough at 1514.

It has no connection with the abridged Book of Assizes printed earlier by Richard Pynson (Beale R47) and later by Richard Tottell (Beale R50, R51), which includes cases from the reigns of Richard II and Henry IV,

V, and VI as well as Edward III (as W.S. Holdsworth pointed out in *Sources and Literature of English Law* (Oxford, 1925), pp. 105-6). Rastell's book treats only the reign of Edward III, presumably of interest because of the continuity implied by a reign that lasted half a century under a king who, as Rastell later wrote, "euer toke hede to the co*m*men welthe of his realme, and ordred and stablysshed his lawes meruelously well."

Evidently it was intended to be the first of a series of major legal works planned by Rastell, to be done with the aid of other lawyers and other printers. National pride and Rastell's concern for it were both involved. After citing Sir John Fortescue's great *De Laudibus Legum Angliae*, he went on to say that he and others had been moved "to take some paine & labour to order this p*r*esent boke," indexing, numbering the cases, and printing it. It is difficult to tell from the preface whether the source was one or several manuscript compilations, or whether "the eyde & helpe of diuers other ge*n*tylme*n*" occurred in the editing and indexing or just in the financing of the project and the printing of the book. The same group was also working on Sir Anthony Fitzherbert's *Grand Abridgment*, already compiled but requiring "the ordering of the kalendars" and "the nomberi*n*g of the cotacions & referment*es* of the cases therin," which Rastell was himself to do. The *Liber Assisarum* and the first of the three volumes of Fitzherbert are all in Rastell's type, and so obviously from his shop; the rest of the *Grand Abridgment* is printed from type belonging to Wynkyn de Worde, whose shop at the Sun in Fleet Street was probably the largest in England, while the woodcut on the title belonged to Richard Pynson, the King's Printer. It seems safe to assume that these two important stationers were associated with Rastell in the *Liber Assisarum* as well, but nothing can be learned about the lawyers or law clerks who might have helped in the preparation of the texts.

It seems certain enough that Rastell himself initiated the projects, encouraged the compilation of the books, and handled the indexing with "figures of algorisme," one of his many interests, which he explained in a special preface.

His prologue in praise of law affirms the preeminence of law in human affairs and the dignity of teaching and studying law, for which the projected books were intended. The commonwealth, he asserted,

> restith nother in incresing of riches power nor honoure but in the incresyng of good maners & condicions of men wherby they may be reducid to knowe god to honoure god to loue god and to lyue in a continuall loue & tranquilyte with theyre neyghbors for the which thing to be atteyned yt ys

to men most expedient to haue ordinancis & lawes for lykwyse as the bry-
del & the spurr directyth & constraineth the hors swyftly & wel to performe hys iourney so doth gode & resonable ordinancis & lawes lede &
direct men to vse gode maners & condicions & therby to honour to drede
& to loue god & verteusly to lyue among theyre neyghbors in continual pes
& tranquilite in firme concord & agrement in an vnite of wil & mynd & in
sensere & Pure loue & charite, which thing deuly to performe ys not gyuen
to mankynde imediatly & only by nature as is gyuen to all other creatours
wich be by nature constreined to do & to lyue after their Kyndis.

Both the large books, he concluded, had been "no smale labour to bryng
to a good fynall conclusion"; where the now complete *Liber Assisarum*
had been "fynisshyd in grete hast," the forthcoming *Grand Abridgment*
was to be "bet*er* done & and with mich more dylyge*n*ce" though it would
contain six to seven hundred leaves of the largest paper.

4   *Grand Abridgment*

Anthony Fitzherbert, *La Graunde Abridgment,* edited and indexed by John Rastell; first volume printed by him, second and third by Wynkyn de Worde, both presumably in partnership with Richard Pynson, 1514-1516, completed 21 December 1516. *2°.* Reprinted by Richard Tottell 1565 (STC 10956) and 1577 (STC 10957).

Title: **Prima pars huius libri.** | [woodcut Hodnett 1507, Beale 7]

Explicit: [at end of third volume, not printed by Rastell] **¶Finis tocius iſtius opis finit' .xxi. die Dicembr | A° dn̄i Milleciſimo quiq̄eteſimo ſextodecimo** | [cut of Royal Arms, Beale 8, used by Pynson]

Collation: 2°, π¹ a⁶ (+π²) b⁶ c⁸ D-V⁸ ²a-²q⁸ ² r⁴, 290 leaves foliated [1] folio. primo **ii-x xi** [omitted in one state] **xii-xlvi lvii xlviii-lxxvii lxxvii** [repeated in one state but usually correct] **lxxviii lxxix-xcv xcvii C.xvii xcviii-ci Cii-Ciiii cv-cvi Cvii-Cxxxviii Cxxxviii C.xxx.ix** [in one state] **Cxl-CC** [blank leaf follows] **CClxxix-CClxxxvii** (=287+1+ two blanks =290), $4 (- ²qr3, ab ²fr4) signed [textura].

RT: follows text with **folio.** in headline from al; sometimes **folio** without point or **fol.**, with the variations implying consistent use of a skeleton forme on one press; e.g. **fol.** $1-4, **folio.** $5-8. It seemed unnecessary to record all these.

Contents: π1: title and woodcut. π1ᵛ:"**Hic ſeq'tur Tabula hui⁹ libri** | A[lombardic cap²]**bbe** .... [two columns to "**¶Finis tabule iſti⁹ Et Incipit liber | magnopere vtilis**". al: "N[init⁶ 26x25]**Ota** ..., text with sections beginning with headings and lombardic caps or initials to ²r4ᵛ; ²f4 and ²q3 blank. There is no formal ending to Rastell's volume; the explicit above occurs on Dd6ᵛ of the third volume; on aal of the third volume, under the title, there is a statement of price which occurs in three different states: "**¶The priſe of this boke .xl.s. whych boke contey= | nyth .iii. great volumes.**", or "**¶The price of the whole boke (.xl.s.) whych. boke conteyneth .iii. great volumes.**", or "**¶The pryſe of the whole boke (.xl.s.) whiche boke conteyneth .iii. great volumes**.". There is no bibliographical significance to these variations, which result from overprinting completed title pages.

Type: text (N4) 57 11., 266 (283) x 180 [215 to sidenotes in outer margin and arabic numerals in gutter], 94 bastard, 93a textura for key words, 116 textura in headings, headlines, and direction lines.

Examined: Bodleian L.4.7.Jur.: British Library 20.e.; Cambridge; Lincoln's Inn . As is common with such large books, many copies have survived; the Graham and Heckel study cited below was based on 23 copies.

Notes: STC 10954; Beale R457-461; Cowley 6; University Microfilms 100.

In the prologue to the *Liber Assisarum*, in which Rastell announced the plan to publish this book, he described it as

> a grete boke of abbregement*es* of arguyd casis rulyd in many yeres of di-
> uers sondry kyngys co*n*teyning .vi or vii leuis of grete pap*er* with diuers
> grete tables lo*n*ging thereto co*n*triuid orderid & no*m*berid with figures of
> algorisme for the grete expedicio*n* & fortherau*n*ce of the stude*n*s of this
> law

and added

> And though that I my self smal of lerni[n]g & discression haue ent*er*-
> priside with the eyde & helpe of diuers other ge*n*tylme*n* & taken labo*ur*s
> & also ente*n*de moo labours to take as wel for the ordering of the kalenders
> of the seyde grete boke of abbrigement*es* as in the nombri*n*g of the cota-
> cions & referment*es* of the cases therin, yet the only prayse of the making
> of the seyd grete abbrigeme*n*t ought to be giuyn to Antony fitzherberd se-
> riant at the law which by his grete and longe study by many yeres con-
> tynuyng hath compylyd and gederyd the same.

W.S. Holdsworth, in *Sources and Literature of English Law* (Oxford, 1925), remarked on the accuracy and extensive research of the work and its use of unpublished Yearbooks and Bracton's Note Book, which made it "a model to future writers of abridgements." L.W. Abbott's *Law Reporting in England 1485-1585* (London, 1973) showed Fitzherbert's dependence on circulating manuscript material, noting that only one entry is dated after 1500-01, the beginning of a break in the Yearbooks series, and that this was "a personal note taken verbally from Justice Frowick."

The most thorough study of this important work is F.L. Boersma's *An Introduction to Fitzherbert's* Abridgement (Abingdon, 1981), a monograph based on his doctoral dissertation. Boersma discusses the practical nature of the work, which abridged case-notes from existing English law books and arranged them for reference in a manner far easier than that of the Yearbooks, which were ordered by terms. While Fitzherbert, Boersma adds, made no use of plea rolls or the records of local or franchisal courts, the book "was decisively the grand abridgement, which swept its forerunners from the field and which holds its own today as a source of English law."

Legal historians of the past seem to have had difficulty with the bibliographical problems the book presents, and there were even those who doubted whether the book was by Fitzherbert. However, all bibliographical difficulties were resolved by Howard Jay Graham and John W. Heckel in "The Book That 'Made' the Common Law: The First Printing of Fitzherbert's 'La Graunde Abridgment,' 1514-1516," *Law Library Journal* 51 (1958), pp. 100-116. After examining some 23 copies, Graham and Heckel demonstrate that there was only one edition before Richard Tottell's reprint of 1565, that variants noted were caused by reprinting of sheets as they came into short supply, and that the type used in the second and third volumes was de Worde's 95 textura, with the s[3] said by Isaac to have been introduced in 1514.

While de Worde was completing the "so besy & so grete a work," Rastell's press was used for a small number of humanist books, all of which may be connected with the More circle, while he himself went on with the compilation of the table to Fitzherbert. The table was published not long before Rastell himself and the printer Thomas Bercula set sail for the New World.

5   *Progymnasmata*

Thomas Linacre, *Progymnasmata*. c.1514. 4° in sixes.

Title: ¶**Linacri progymnasmata | Grammatices vulgaria.**

Colophon: ¶**Empryntyd in London̄ on y̆ ſowth ſyde of | paulys by Iohn̄ Raſtell with y̆ priuylege | of our moſt ſuuerayn lord kyng Henry | the. viii. grauntyd to the compyler | therof. that noo man in thys hys | realme ſell none but ſuch as the | ſame cōpyler makyth pryn= | tyd for yͤ ſpace of ii. yeere**.

Collation: 4°, a-f⁶ g⁴, 40 unnumbered leaves; $3 (-g2, 3) signed [textura].

Contents: al: title. al^V: Latin dedicatory verses by Thomas Linacre, Thomas More, and William Lily. a2: "T[lombardic cap²]Here ...". text with headings, each section beginning with a paragraph mark, to f4^V. On f4^V: "¶**IDIOMATA VERBORVM.**" to gl^V. g2: "¶**Erroris** [stet] **quorūdam in hoc opuſcule Re= | cognito.**" to g3. g3^V: blank. g4: colophon. g4^V: [device McKerrow 37, with break in upper border and what seems to be faulty inking at right].

Type: text (b3) 30 11., 114 (139) x 93, 93a textura, title 116 textura.

Examined: British Library G.7569.

Notes: STC 15635; University Microfilms 59. The state of the device suggests that the book should be dated from 1514, while the address shows it to be before 1517.

Presumably this is the Latin grammar that Linacre had written for St. Paul's School and that John Colet had rejected in 1511. The rejection angered Linacre, and Erasmus attempted to pacify both humanists in the autumn of that year (*Collected Works of Erasmus* 227). Rastell's publication of the book with prefatory verses by More and William Lily, who was headmaster of Colet's new school from its foundation in 1512, was probably also intended to patch up a rift within a group of very close friends. Lily's verse implies that there had been an earlier edition or circulated manuscript under a false name, containing many errors, a further reason why he and More would wish Rastell to print Linacre's.

The two-year royal privilege is Linacre's, not Rastell's.

6   Donatus, *Devotions*

Anonymous, *Donatus Devotionis*. c. 1514-1516. 8°.

Incipit: ¶**Incipit prologus de ora | tione ſuper donatum. deuo= | tionis.**
[row of type orn 4x44]

Explicit and colophon: ¶**Explicit donatus deuotionis de octo   /   ptib**[9]
oͬrois. Impreſſū p̄ Iohez raſtel 2 mo | ranter auſtrali p̱te ecclesͤie
ſancti pauli.

Collation: 8°, a-1[8], 88 unnumbered leaves; $2 (+bc3) signed, al as Al
[textura].

Contents: al: incipit [woodcut, Christ raising Lazarus, 30x27, inset seven
lines] E[lombardic cap[2]]V̄agelica ..." to a4. On a4: table of contents. a4[v]:
[woodcut Hodnett 2284] | "¶**Deuotio quid eſt: & de ſex acci | dentib**[9]
deuotioni. De quib[9] **pu | ritas, eſt prima particula. |** P[lombardic
cap[2]]**Artes...**", text under 33 headings, each beginning with lombardic
cap[2] or [3], to 18[v]: explicit.

Type: Text (al) 23 11., 108 (111) x 75, 93a textura, headings 116 textura
in incipit, opening of preface, and a4[v].

Examined: Cambridge Syn. 8.52.42, Royal Library copy.

Notes: STC 7018.7; Sayle 348; University Microfilms 1135. The date is
uncertain, though obviously before 1517; the publication of the book as
a guide to learning and Christian piety relates it to that of the *Progymnasmata,* and its publication is probably of about the same time.

The crowded octavo design, which is very different from that of other
Rastell books, seems to be intended to suggest a similarity to the familiar
Donat from which people learned their basic grammar. The text itself follows the pattern of the Donatus, but arranges spiritual quotations under
the grammatical headings. Rastell's edition consists only of Book I. The
book was compiled in the early fifteenth century, and had wide manuscript circulation in England and on the Continent.

See A.I. Doyle, "The European Circulation of Three Latin Spiritual
Texts" in *Latin and Vernacular*, ed. A.J. Minnis (Cambridge, 1989), pp.
126-41, especially pp. 138-141.

7   *Fulgens and Lucrece*

Henry Medwall, *Here is conteyned a godely interlude of Fulgens Cenatoure of Rome. Lucres his doughter. Gayus flaminius. & Publius. Cornelius.* c. 1514-1516. 4° in sixes.

Title:¶**Here is cōteyned a godely interlude of Fulgens | Cenatoure of Rome. Lucres his doughter. Gayus | flaminius. & Publi⁹. Corneli⁹. of the diſputacyon of | noblenes. & is deuyded in two ptyes/ to be played at | ii. tymes. Cōpyled by mayſter Henry medwall. late | chapelayne to yᵉ ryght reuerent fader in god Iohan | Morton cardynall & Archebyſſop of Caūterbury.** | [woodcut Hodnett 2288]

Colophon: ¶ **Emprynted at london by Iohan raſtell | dwellynge on the ſouth ſyde of paulys | chyrche by ſyde paulys cheyne.**

Collation: 4°, a-f⁶, 40 unnumbered leaves, $3 (-fl, g3) signed [textura]

Contents: al: title (verso blank). a2: "**Intrat A dicens.** | A[lombardic cap²] **For goddis ...**", text to d6ᵛ, "**¶Finis prime partis**". el:¶ **Intrat A dicens** | M[lombardic cap³] **Vche gode ...**", text to g3ᵛ:colophon.

Type: (c3) 33 ll., 152 (158) x 105; 93a textura.

Examined: British Library C.60.h.19, British Library fragment e3.4 (formerly Bagford fragment, Harleian MS 5919, f. 20, no. 28), note uncorrected state of e(i); Huntington 62599, wanting g4, said by Greg to have survived as a fragmentary blank until the book was rebound after 1919 (Mostyn sale 1919; see also A.W. Reed, "Fulgens and Lucrece," *TLS* 898 (1919), p. 178).

Notes: STC 17778; University Microfilms 124; Greg 1, 2. Greg's argument that the book must be dated before 1517 by its address is most certainly correct. The Bagford fragment was edited by Greg in the Malone Society *Collections,* Vol. I Part 2 (Oxford, 1908), pp. 137-142, and a photographic facsimile appeared in *Materialen zur Kunde des alteren Englischen Dramas* 12 (1905), pp. 100-104. After the complete text appeared at the Mostyn sale, the complete text was issued in facsimile by Seymour de Ricci (New York, 1920); it was edited by F.S. Boas and A.W. Reed (Oxford, 1926) and by F.S. Boas in *Five Pre-Shakespearean Comedies* (Oxford, 1934), pp. 1-72; by Edmund Creeth in *Tudor Plays* (New York, 1966), pp. 1-70, notes pp. 537-41; by A.H. Nelson in *The Plays of Henry Medwall* (Cambridge, 1980), pp. 31-89, notes pp. 173-92; and by P. Meredith (Leeds, 1981).

The woodcut Hodnett 2288 on the title page was studied by Robert Mullally in "The Source of the *Fulgens* Woodcut," *Theatre Notebook,* 30

(1976), pp. 61-65, in which it was shown that Rastell's version was a reversed copy of a cut used by Michael Toulouse and Denis Millier at Paris in about 1490.

Like Rastell's other books at this period, this play text came from within the More circle, in this case from the household of Cardinal Morton where More had received his early education and, as William Roper records, had taken part in plays, and where Medwall had been a chaplain. It is the first published English drama, and one of the first secular English plays, and perhaps the first in which a woman has an important role to play. The theme of real worth and whether it is found in birth or in goodness and achievement reflects the concerns of More and Rastell, as seen in the *Utopia*, the law prefaces, and the later play *Of Gentylnes and Nobylyte*.

8   *Commendations of Matrimony*

William Harrington, *In thys boke are conteyned the commendacions of matrimony.* c.1514-1517. 4° in sixes. Reprinted by Rastell (9) and by John Skot for himself and Robert Redman, 24 July 1528 (STC 12799 and 12800).

Title: [most of the top missing] **contractyn | in the ſame. Wi | ſuch impedimētes as | trimony to be made. And | teyne other thynges whyche | curates be boundē by the la= | we to declare often- tymes | to their pariſhens. Em | prented at the inſtaū | ce of mayſter poly= | dore vergil arche | deaken of we= | les.**

Explicit and colophon: **¶Here endith the boke very prou | fitable for euery body to rede or he | re red which is called the ryghte | way of matrimoni. Emprented at london by fore the ſouthe dore | of paulis ₥ me Iohāne Raſtell.**

Collation: 4°, $A^6 b^4$ c-d^6, 22 unnumbered leaves; $3 (-bc2, Ab3) signed textura.

Contents: A1: title. A1^V: Latin dedication to Polydore Vergil. A2: "F[lombardic cap2]OR THE INSTRVCtion ...", text to d6, with wood-cut table of consanguinity on b2^V, table of affinity on b4, and table of spiritual cognation on c2. On d6: explicit and colophon. d6^V: within a frame of ornamental strips left 15 over woodcut Hodnett 2087, top 2 with two type orns, right 14 over two woodcuts of the 23x23 series, lower 11 and two type orns: [device McKerrow 37] | [device McKerrow 40].

Type: text (el) 38 11., 176 (181) x 98, 93a textura, title, headings, and colophon 116 textura.

Examined: Bodleian Douce H.212.

Notes: STC 12798.5 (12801); Dibdin 850; the earlier edition with side-notes, unnumbered chapters, and no table, with the table of consanguin-ity taken to seven places, despite the note that "after *th*e iiii. degree is none *im*pediment". The 24 July 1528 reprint by John Skot is a line-for-line reprint.

The title indicates that the book was written at the instance of Polydore Vergil, who had suggested the need for a book of marriage rules based on both canon law and provincial constitutions for the use of parish priests. Harrington, a friend of Vergil and presumably like him a friend of More and the Christian humanist group, probably began work on the book in 1512, the year in which Vergil resumed his position as Collector of Peter's Pence in England, an office which gave him authority on marriage contracts within questionable degrees.

The fact that a slightly smaller and less expensive reprint followed, with the tables of consanguinity and affinity cut off at five places, the sidenotes deleted from the statement of matrimonial impediments, and a table of numbered chapters added, implies some success for the book. The Skot and Redman reprint of 1528 has the tables at seven places.

Four copies of this book were in the inventory of the Sign of the Sun in 1553, but it seems impossible to say what edition they were. See H.R. Plomer, "An Inventory of Wynkyn de Worde's House 'The Sun in Fleet Street' in 1553," *The Library* 3rd ser., 11 (1915), pp. 228-234.

9   *Commendations of Matrimony*

[another edition] William Harrington, *In thys boke are conteyned the commendacions of matrimony*, c.1514-1517. 4° in eights.

Title: ¶In thys boke are conteyned the comenda= | cions of matri- mony the maner & forme of | contractyng ſolepniſſyng & lyuyng in | the ſame with the declaracio of all | ſuch impedimentis as doth let | matrimony to be made & alſo | certeyn other thigis whi= | che curates be bounde by | the lawe to declare of= | tetymes to theyre ꝑi= | ſhes. Empreted at | the iſtauce of ma= | ſter polydore v̄= | gil archede= | akene of welles

Explicit and colophon: ¶Here endith the boke very profi= | table for euery body to rede or here re | de whyche is called the ryght waye | of matrimony. Empreted at london | ꝑ me Iohane Raſtell

Collation: 4°, A⁴ B-C⁸ D⁴, 24 unnumbered leaves; $4 (-AD3, 4) signed [textura].

Contents: A1: title. A1ᵛ: Latin dedication to Polydore Vergil. A2: "F[lombardic cap²]Or The Inſtruccyon ...", text to D3ᵛ, with woodcut table of consanguinity on B5, table of affinity on B6, and table of spiri- tual cognation on C1. On D3ᵛ: "¶Here folowith the table of thys | preſent boke" | text to D4: explicit and colophon | [device McKerrow 40]. D4⁴: [within a frame of ornamental strips left 8 top 12, right 6 lower 4 justified by type ornament and asterisk at left and right device McKer- row 37].

Type: text (A4), 3 11., 143 x 106; 93a textura.

Examined: Durham University Library Bamburgh Select III, examined for me by Dr. A.I. Doyle.

Notes: STC 12798.7, edition with numbered chapters and table, side- notes deleted, and tables reduced to five places from the seven of the ear- lier edition. See *Catalogue of the Library at Bamburgh Castle* 2 (London, 1859), p. 68.

10   *Tabula*

Anthony Fitzherbert and John Rastell, *Tabula libri magni abbreuia-menti.* 10 February 1517. 2°.

Explicit: ¶**Tabula libri magni abbreuiamenti | libroru̅ legum anglo-rum finit felicit° im | preſſ. londini impenſis et industria Io= | hannis Raſtell Anno.dni.M.CCCC | xvij.die.x. Februarii.**

Collation: 2°, a-c^8 d^6 e^8 f^6 g-i^8 k^6 l-n^8 o^6 p^4 ^{2}a-p^8 ^{2}q^{10} A-L^8 M^6, 332 unnumbered leaves; $4 (-^{2}a^{2}kAl, p3, dfkopM4; +^{2}q5) signed, missigning G4 as F2 [textura, second lower case alphabet bastard].

Contents: al: "**Tabula prime partis magni abbreuiame̅ti libroru̅ legu̅ angloru̅**" | [ornamental strip 14 justified at right by four type ornaments] | "**¶Prologus Iohi̅s Raſtell. | ¶Haud ...**", text to "**¶Explicit prologus**". al^v: : "**Prefatiu*n*cula Iohi̅s Raſtell hui^9 Tabule ordine̅ manifeſtas**" | [explanation of indexing method followed by index in three columns for first volume]. a2: "**Abbe prior p̲ſon eueſq̲ dean ou maſſ de colege |** E[lombardic cap^2]N...", text in two columns with sections beginning lombardic cap^2 to p4. p4^v: blank. ^{2}al: "**Tabula ſecunde p̲tis magni | abbreuiamenti libroru̅ legu̅ angloru̅**" | [woodcut Hodnett *2286^a]. ^{2}al^v: "**Tabula ſecunde p̲tis** | index as above to ^{2}a2: "**Damage | D**[lom-bardic cap^2]**Ouble ... ,'** text as above to ^{2}q9^v. On ^{2}q9^{vb}: "**fiuis** [stet] ſecunde partis". ^{2}q10^{r-v}: blank. A1: "**¶Tabula tercie partis abbreuiame̅ti libroru̅ legu̅ Angloru̅**" | [woodcut Hodnett *2286a]. A1^v: "**Tabula tercie partis**" | [index as above to] "**¶Finis Tabule**". A2: "**Obligicion | O** [init 16x17]**Vt ...,**" text as above to M6vb: explicit.

Type: text (kl) 2 columns of 42 11., 194 (210) x 151, each column 71, 93a textura, 94 bastard, 84 bastard, headings 116 textura.

Examined: Bodleian Vet.A.1.d.2.; British Library C.69.g.6.; Cambridge Syn.4.51.2; Harvard Beale R462.

Notes: STC 10955; Beale R462; Cowley 7; Sayle 344; University Micro-films 101. This appears to have been the last book printed at Paul's Chain. Rastell sailed on his frustrated voyage to the New World in the early summer of 1517, after receiving a letter of recommendation from the King on 5 March 1516-17; these dates suggest that the Fitzherbert book was forward dated, and that the 10 February was actually in 1516-17.

As Boersma argued in his *Introduction to Fitzherbert's Abridgement*, the idea of an index to make the vast amount of material in the book available fairly easily was probably Fitzherbert's. Rastell states in the *Prefatiun-*

cula that Fitzherbert had assembled a calendar for the *Abridgment*, but adds that he himself had worked on the first part, that corresponding to the volume his house had printed.

Through the *Tabula* the titles of cases from Fitzherbert appear at the left with the signatures of the leaves on which they appear, followed by "the accio*ns* namis whe*re th*e seid casis be arguid if ther be any markid" and the terms and regnal year, which made the work a guide to the Yearbooks as well as to Fitzherbert. According to Boersma the *Tabula* "contained 247 titles, 5654 subtitles, and 31982 citations, or more than two citations for every case in *La Graunde Abridgment*" (p. 39).

Besides the English *Prefatiuncula* explaining the system, Rastell also prefixed his *Prologus* to discuss the nature of law, its overwhelming importance in human affairs, and its tripartite nature as divine, human, and natural law, a distinction he was to make many times through the rest of his career:

> Et cum homo tam animal rationale quam naturale existens & ad simili-
> tudinem diuinam formatur ille ergo precepta legis diuine obseruans premi-
> um legis diuine obtinebit at pro preceptis legis humane eiusdem legis
> premium co*n*sequetur. Sed sollumodo viuendo secundum nature lege*m*
> tantemodo mors fine superueniet. Igitur non solum homini conuenit legis
> nature vti preceptis sed etiam tam precepta legis diuine qu*am* humane dil-
> igenter obseruare per qu*o*d vite mundane tranqu*i*llitate ac eterna felicitate
> fruet*ur*.

After the publication of the *Tabula* Rastell and a group of associates completed arrangements for the New World expedition and Rastell sailed, accompanied by Thomas Bercula, a printer who must have been employed in the Paul's Chain shop.

11   *Abridgment of Statutes*

John Rastell, *Abridgement of Statutes* (to 1 Henry VII, i.e. 30 October 1485-1486). 25 October 1519. 8°. Reprinted in expanded form by Rastell (43), and, further expanded, by William Rastell (52).

Explicit: ¶Adeſt finis p̄ tēpore preſenti | Thus ēdyth ẙ abbreuiacōn of ſtatutſ traſlatvd | out of frēch ito ēgliſh by Iohn̄ Raſtell. & ipritid | by ẙ ſame Iohn̄ ẙ xxv day of october in ẙ xj vere | of yᵉ reyn of our ſouereyn lord kyng hēry the viij | wyth ẙ pryuylege of our ſeyd ſouerei lord grau̅= | tyd to ẙ seyd Iohn that no nother imprit ageyn | thys ſeyd work nor no nother ellſ | where prin= | tyd of them ſell wythin this realme duryng the | ſpace of vij yerſ next after this furſt inpreſſion.

Collation: 8°, πA^4 A-N^8 O^4, 112 unnumbered leaves; $3 (-$\pi$AAO2, πAAGHO3, $F) signed [textura, πA lombardic cap].

Contents: A1: "¶The ſtatutes | **Prohemium Iohānis Raſtell** | B[lombardic cap²]ecauſe ...," text to π. πA3^V: "**The kalendar** | **¶Accyons popular**," text in two columns to πA4^V. A1: "¶**Accion popular**. | I[lombardic cap²]f ...," text to O4: explicit. O4^V: [device McKerrow 37].

Type: text (c3) 26 11., 120 (125) x 86, 93a textura, headings and first line of explicit 116 textura.

Examined: British Library BE 11/1.

Notes: STC 9515.5; Cowley 8; Dibdin 830. This seems the earlier of the two books in octavo printed in late 1519 to early 1520. Both the *Statutes* and the *Interlude* were Rastell's own work; both combine his concern for the necessity of law with a newly-declared concern for the primacy of the English language; both are rather cramped and graceless in design and seem rather carelessly printed. Coincidentally each survives in a unique copy at the British Library, and, although they came from different sources, the two books were once bound together.

The *Statutes* appeared on 25 October, less than a month after Michaelmas, when Rastell's lease of the house from the Bridge House Masters took effect, and less than a month before he opened his case against John Ravyn, the purser who had caused the failure of the New World expedition.

Rastell's preface first treated the development of the English language into one that could comprehend the subtleties of law. In earlier times, he argued, the use of the Conqueror's French had begun to diminish, so wise men had caused "matters of law *and* accions betwen *partes*" to be heard in court in English and entered in the rolls in Latin, while the statutes themselves remained in French, even those the people needed to know. Such outmoded customs had been abolished by Henry VII, who perceived that English had been "maruelously ame*n*dyd & augmentyd" and that translation from other languages had caused "mych more plenty & habou*n*daunce off englysh," which made the language "suffycyent of hyt self to expown any lawys or ordynancys," and had therefore ordered the statutes from his first year to be kept in English. Rastell had then decided to abridge all statutes containing penalties into English, even those that actually were in English from the Tudor accession.

The primary concern of the preface was, of course, to argue the need for knowledge of the law and of further aids to legal education. The reader was naturally warned that anyone with a legal problem should "resorte to some man *tha*t ys lernyd in the laws of thys realme."

The "neclygens of the prynters" that Rastell warned his readers of is demonstrated in the printing of signature L, in which the compositor has imposed two pages (2 and 3) incorrectly into the outer rather than the inner forme, and put 4 and 5 into the inner forme. Such an error was easily made, since the text has neither catchwords nor running titles, and the sheet largely consists of statute law about the Severn and the Staple, so the compositor was without headings or numberings to show the sequence of type pages. The inner forme seems to have been reversed on the bed of the press as well. This error or series of errors was probably corrected in other copies of the book, but none is known to have survived.

Finally, the Father of Heaven device shows damage in this book for the first time, a weakening of the impression of the left thumb of the Creator, apparently caused by simple wear. It can be seen in the device to the end of Rastell's printing career, though it never got worse.

12   *The Interlude of the Four Elements*

John Rastell, *A new interlude and a mery of the nature of the .iiij. ele-mentes. c.1520. 8°.*

Title: ¶A new iuterlude [sic] and a mery of the | nature of the .iiij. ele-mentʃ declarynge many pro | per poyntʃ of phyloʃophy naturall" and of dyuers | ʃtraunge landys | and of dyuers ʃtraunge effectʃ & | cau-ʃis" whiche interlude yf y̆ hole matter be playd | wyl conteyne the ʃpace of an hour and a halfe" but | yf ye lyʃt ye may leue out muche of the ʃad mater | as the meʃʃengers p̲te" and ʃome of naturys parte | and ʃome of experyens p̲te & yet the matter wyl de | pend conueny-ently | and than it wyll not be paʃte | thre quarters of an hour of length. | ¶Here folow the namys of the pleyers. | ¶ The meʃʃengere | Nature naturate | Humanyte Studyous deʃire / senʃuall appetyte / The tauerner / Experyence / yngnoraunce / Also yf ye lyʃt ye may brynge in a dyʃgyʃynge. | ¶Here folow dyuers matters whiche be in | this interlude conteynyd. | [text running on to A1^V].

Collation: 8°, A- [G?]^8, 56 [?] unnumbered leaves; $4 (-A4, B2, 3; +A1) signed [textura].

Contents: A1: title. with text running on to A1^V. A2: "¶The meʃʃenger. | T[lombardic cap^2]Haboūdant grace ..." to A4^V: "¶Hic intrat natura naturata Huma= | nyte & Studyous deʃire portas figurā | ¶Natura Naturata| T[lombardic cap^2]He ...," text to end with characters named in full in centered headings until B2^V, after which most headings are in the left margin. On E4^V: a dance with a blank musical stave. E5: part song with music to E6. On E7 a blank musical stave. The surviving copy ends at E8^V, but the original probably went to $G, to allow space for a resolu-tion and a festive ending; and certainly must have included a colophon or explicit and, given the nature of the text, device McKerrow 37.

Type: text (A3) 26 11., 121 (125) x 89, 93a textura, headings and first line of title 116 textura, music stave about 15 x 85 to 90.

Examined: British Library C.39.b.17, from the Garrick collection, with B1-3, E1-2, 8 slightly defective; wanting $D and all after E8.

Notes: STC 20722; Dibdin 849; Greg 6; University Microfilms 140. The text was issued in facsimile by John S. Farmer, Tudor Facsimile Texts (London and Edinburgh, 1908; repr. New York, 1970); it was edited in part by A.W. Pollard in *English Miracle Plays* (London, 1895), pp. 97-105; by Brooke Crutchley in *Siberch Celebrations* (Cambridge, 1979), pp. 81-113; and by Richard Axton, in *Three Rastell Plays* (Cam-bridge, 1979), pp. 29-68.

The *Interlude*, as noted above, is close to the English *Statutes* in format, general appearance or design, and theme; obviously both were done or overseen by the same workman at about the same time. As mentioned above, the surviving copies were once bound together.

The single-impression music printing in the *Interlude*, presumably invented either by Rastell or an employee, has received some scholarly attention. Robert Steele argued in *The Earliest English Music Printing* (London, 1903), pp. 5-6, and again in "A Note on 'A New Interlude'," *The Library,* 4th series, 9 (1928), pp. 90-91, that the music printing indicated that the play was printed in about 1539 by John Gough, who did in fact use the notes in the 1530s. His view was rejected by F.S. Isaac in his examination of Rastell's types and by W.W. Greg in "Notes on Some Early Plays," *The Library*, 4th series, 11 (1930), pp. 46-50. A. Hyatt King's close study of the book and his unrivalled knowledge of music printing have resulted in a series of valuable discussions: a brief caption in *Four Hundred Years of Music Printing* (London, 1964), Plate XI; an examination of the relationship between the extant copies of the *Interlude* and the *Statutes* in "Rastell Reunited," *Essays in Honour of Victor Scholderer*, ed. Dennis E. Rhodes (Mainz, 1970), pp. 213-8; and "The Significance of John Rastell in Early Music Printing," *The Library,* 5th ser. 26 (1972), pp. 197-214. Besides his solution to the problem of the music printing, he has also shown that the song sung by the vice Sensual Appetite and his friends in the interlude is a musical parody of a four-part song current in about 1520, suggesting that the production and publication of the play would have occurred when the parody was topical.

Rastell's authorship of the play, which is anonymous, is attested to by both John Bale and John Pits, and made even more certain by the subject of the four elements, already summarized in the larger printer's device, by the knowledge of North America, the complimentary reference to "Irelande that holsome grounde," and the concerns for service to the commonwealth, the rule of law, the importance of moral teaching, and the excellence of the English language.

The *Interlude* has also had much attention from scholars concerned with its geography, for it is the earliest English discussion of the New World and apparently the first English work to call it America. The most important question clearly is the source of Rastell's cosmographical knowledge, which seems to be a combination of Amerigo Vespucci's *Quattuor Navigationes* and first-hand accounts from travellers—exactly the same combination found in his brother-in-law's more famous *Utopia*. The next is what Studious Desire has with him when he enters the stage "portans figuram," apparently a figure or diagram to be used by Natura Naturata to explain the structure of the cosmos and the nature of the four elements. It seems to be used again when Studious Desire explains the rotundity of the earth to a very skeptical Humanity and also to be used in Experience's lecture:

> Syr as for all suche questyons
> Of townes to know the sytuacyon
> How ferre they be a sunder
> And other poyntes of cosmogryphy
> ye shall neuer lerne then [sic] more surely
> Then by that fugure [sic] yonder
> For who that fygure dyd fyrst deuyse
> It semeth well he was wyse
> And perfyte in this seyens
> For bothe the se and lande also
> Lye trew and iust as they sholde do
> I know by experyens.

The text implies pretty clearly the mixture of science and talk with sailors and explorers, as well as the urgent need to understand nature and her workings. Studious Desire, who I take it actually carried it on stage, says that the figure was left for Humanity's instruction by "lorde nature." There were copies of "mappis of Europa" in Rastell's shop after his death (Roberts 3), and it seems reasonable to assume that he would probably have published a Mappa Mundi. But the figure on the stage must have been large enough for demonstration to an audience, and was probably drawn specifically for the staging of the interlude.

M.E. Borish argued in "Source and Intention of *The Four Elements*," *Studies in Philology* 25 (1938), pp. 149-63, that Rastell's main source was Gregorius Reisch's *Margarita Philosophica* in the 1515 Strasburg edition, establishing a link between that book's map and Rastell's cosmography, particularly in the use of the terms India Major and India Minor. George B. Parks, in "The Geography of the *Interlude of the Four Elements*," *Philological Quarterly* 27 (1938), pp. 251-62, also felt that the map from Reisch was the most likely source, but felt it more probable that Rastell used an early navigator's map and that much of his geographical knowledge was simply hearsay. Indeed, he concluded that Rastell was unaware of most of the advances in cosmographical knowledge that had been published before his voyage, including Vespucci's tract, which looms so large in Utopia.

In "Sources of John Rastell's *The Nature of the Four Elements*," *PMLA* 57 (1942), pp. 77-88, Elizabeth M. Nugent produced an ingenious set of parallel texts intended to prove that the sources were Reisch, Martin Waldseemüller's *Cosmographiae Introductio* (Strasburg, 1507 and later editions), William Caxton's *Mirror of the World* (Westminster, 1481), the *De Proprietatibus Rerum* of Bartholomeus Anglicus as translated by John of Trevisa (Westminster, 1495), and John Sacrobosco's *Textus de Sphaera* (Paris, 1511 and later editions). Parks agreed in a reply, "Rastell and Waldseemüller's Map," *PMLA* 58 (1943), pp. 572-4, but insisted that the figure on the stage must have been "highly simplified." Axton, the play's most recent editor, felt that Rastell used the gigantic *Carta Marina* of Waldseemüller, printed in 1516 (pp. 6-7).

Douglas Leechman noted in "John Rastell and the Indians," *Queen's Quarterly* 51 (1944), pp. 73-7, that Rastell's account of North American natives was remarkably accurate, and assumed that he had drawn much from Bristol mariners, who were familiar with the fishing banks and coniferous forests of the north, whereas Vespucci had confined himself to the tropics.

Some further sources were suggested by Johnstone Parr in "More Sources for Rastell's *Interlude of the Four Elements*," *PMLA* 60 (1945), pp. 48-58, and "John Rastell's Geographical Knowledge of America, " *Philological Quarterly* 27 (1948), pp. 229-40, in which he disagreed sharply with Parks and asserted that Rastell's knowledge was extremely good.

Besides the combination of concerns mentioned above as indicating Rastell's authorship of the interlude, there is also a reference to his frustrated voyage:

> But yet not longe a go
> Some men of this countrey went
> By the kynges noble consent
> It for to serche to that entent
> And coude not be brought therto
> But they that were they [sic] venteres
> Haue cause to curse their maryners
> Fals of promys and dissemblers
> That falsely them be trayed
> Which wolde take no paine to saile farther
> Than their owne lyst and pleasure
> Wherfore that vyage and dyuers other
> Suche katyffes haue distroyed.

Lost through their dishonesty was the glory that would have come to England if Englishmen had taken possession of the New World, made the first buildings there, extended the king's "domynyon," and taught true religion, civilized ways of life, and valuable manual trades to the natives.

13   *Old Tenures*

Anonymous. *The Tenuris*. Law French with English translation by John Rastell. c.1524. 2°. Reprinted by Rastell c.1525 (16).

No title; text begins on A1 under centred heading "**T**[lombardic cap]**he Tenuris**". Colophon: **Impreſſum Cum priuilegio | regali**

Collation: 2°, A⁶ B⁴, 10 unnumbered leaves; $3 (-B3, +A1) signed [textura].

Contents: A1 heading | text in two columns, left Law French, right English, each beginning with a two-line lombardic capital **T**, after which sections begin with paragraph marks, to B4: left column "**¶Finis**"; right column "**¶Finis**" | centered colophon. B4^v: within a frame of ornamental strips, left six woodcuts of the 23x23 series and one at the base of the 23x14 series, upper three woodcuts of the 23x23 series, right 15, lower 5, 155x115 enclosing 114x73 [device McKerrow 37].

Type: text (B2) 40 11., 187 (191) x 133; Law French column 186x51; English column 187x76; Law French 94 bastard, English 93a textura, heading and colophon 116 textura.

Examined: Cambridge Syn. 5.52.2; Cambridge, King's M.33.56.

Notes: STC 23879.7; Beale T71; Dibdin 858; University Microfilms 1804. Both copies are bound with copies of the *Terms* (14).

There is no solid evidence for the dating of this or the *Terms*. Both obviously were printed at about the same time, seemingly after 1520, when the royal privilege became common, and before 1525, when the large device developed a break at its base. Their typographic style is very different from that of the *Statutes* and *Interlude*.

The evidence which suggests that Rastell was himself the translator is found in three points: his specific interest in legal education at the time; the likelihood that these books were published with some kind of agreement with Pynson, who as King's Printer held at least nominally a monopoly of law books; and the fact that he was the compiler of the *Terms*.

14   *Terms*

John Rastell, *Exposiciones Terminorum Legum Anglorum.* Law French and English, preface by Rastell. c.1524. 2°. Reprinted by Rastell c.1525 to 1527 (17), again c.1525 to 1527 (34), Law French only 15 July 1527 (36); by Richard Tottell 29 April 1563 (STC 20703.5 and five later editions). Entered to Tottell 18 February 1582-83 along with Rastell's other law copies (Arber II.419), and finally became part of the Stock of the Stationers' Company, after passing through the hands of Charles Yetsweirt, Clerk of the Signet and common law text patentee, who published it in 1595 (STC 20709). Further editions followed down to 1742; see these in Cowley 10, 20, 51, 58, 63, 68, 74, 88, 90, 94, 100, 103, 107, 111, 115, 119, 122, 126, 127, 130, 131, 145, 158, 163, 177, 195, 208, 237.

No title; text begins on A1 under paragraph headings as follows: Latin title between woodcuts of the 23x14 series: "E[lombardic cap^2]Xpoſi-cioes ſ̄mior' legū anglor'. Et na | tura breuiū cū diuerſibȝ caſibȝ regu | lis et fundametis legum tam de libris Ma= | giſtri Litteltoni quā de aliis legum libris | collectis & breuit° compilatis p̄ Iuuinibȝ valde nec-eſſa= | riis." [row of type ornaments 3x91] | English title also between woodcuts of the 23x14 series: "T[lombardic cap^2] He expoſicions of ẙ termys of ẙ law of england & | the nature of the writtſ with diuers rulys & prin= | cipalles of the law" as well out of the bokis of mayſter lit= | telton as of other bokis of the law gaderyd and breuely | compy-lyd for yong men very neceſſarye."

Colophon: **¶Inpryntyed at london in Chepeſyde at Powles gate. | ¶Cum priuilegio regali.**

Collation: 2°, A^8 B-F^6 G^4, 42 unnumbered leaves; $3 (-G3; +A4) signed [textura with arabic numerals, except in G, where the numerals are roman].

Contents: A1: headings and table in three columns to A1^V. A2: [row of type ornaments 4x30] "**¶Prologus Iohīs Raſtell.**" [row of type ornaments] | "**¶Lyke wyſe as ...**" to A2^V. A3: text in two columns, left Law French and right English, each beginning with two-line lombardic cap A, after which each item begins with a paragraph mark, to G4: explicit under Law French column, "**¶Thus endyth this boke | for this preſent tyme.**"; explicit under English column, "**¶Adeſt huius libri finis pro | tempore preſenti**" | colophon | [device McKerrow 40]. G4^V [within a frame of ornamental strips, left 3, upper 13, right 2, lower 10, 134x94 enclosing 108x73, device McKerrow 37].

Type: text (A2) 40 11., 187 (193) x 130; Law French column 187x51; English column 187x75; Law French 94 bastard, English 93a textura, headings, first line of preface, and first line of English text 116 textura.

Examined: Cambridge Syn. 5.52.2; Cambridge, King's M.56.

STC 20701; Beale T452; Cowley 20; Sayle 352; University Microfilms 1493. Both copies are bound with copies of the *Old Tenures* (13). The book is self-evidently identical to the *Tenures* in design and intention, completing the series of legal education books at least for the time being.

Notes: Rastell's preface characteristically uses the law of nature "whych compellyth euery thyng to do his kind" to argue that society also needs clear and consistent law. Knowledge of the law, he argues further, was necessary to prevent wrongs from being done and to create unity among the people. English people should know the English law, and so Rastell has taken it upon himself "to declare and to expown certyn obscure and derke termys consernyng the lawis of thys realme" for the sake of young students.

15   *Hundred Merry Tales*

Anonymous, possibly John Rastell, *A .C. Mery Tales. c.1524-25. 2°.* Reprinted by Peter Treveris for Rastell 22 November 1526 and by Robert Copland (?) c.1548 (STC 23664.5). Later entered to John Walley in 1557-58 (Arber I.75), to John Charlwood on 15 January 1582 as formerly the property of Sampson Awdely (Arber II.405), and finally to James Roberts on 28-31 May 1594 (Arber II.651). None of these survives even in fragmentary form.

Title: within a frame of ornamental strips, left 5, upper missing, right 6, lower 12, enclosing at top two woodcuts of the 23x23 series | ornamental strip 4 | ¶ **A, C, mery** | **Talys.** | row of type ornaments | two woodcuts of the 23x23 series.

Colophon: [fragment] **booke of a. C mery | ondon at the ſygne of | gate next** | [to left ornamental strip 12 over a woodcut of the 23x14 series; device McKerrow 37; to right ornamental strip 13] | ¶**Cum priuilegio. | Regali.**

Collation: 2°, A-F^4, 24 leaves foliated [1-2] **i** [copy is imperfect, with foliation missing to 5, which is arabic] 6 [rest of foliation is missing]; $2 signed [textura].

RT: **Fol.** [on rectos].

Contents: A1: title. A1^v: [calendar, with heading missing, single column to A2^v]. A3 "**A** [initial^7 31x32] **Certayne Curate** ...", text with each of the hundred tales beginning with text cap^2 or ^{3}, morals beginning with paragraph marks, to F4. F4^v: colophon.

Type: text (B1) 41 11., 190 (198) x 128, 93a textura, title and privilege 220 textura, first line of colophon 116 textura.

Examined: British Library Huth 31 (imperfect); Nash fragments, now in BL (D2.3 with some minor press variation).

Notes: STC 23663; University Microfilms 1397. The Huth copy in the British Library is very imperfect, especially about the edges; presumably it is the one made up from waste sheets from several copies by J.J. Conybeare in about 1815, and edited by S.W. Singer. This emended text was edited by W. Carew Hazlitt in *Shakespeare's Jest-Books,* 1 (London, 1864), pp. i-x, v-xii, ll. 12-129, 130-132. Both editors seem primarily interested in the possibility that Shakespeare knew and used the compilation. However, it seems not unlikely that the charge that Beatrice in *Much Ado About Nothing* had her good wit out of the *Hundred Merry*

Tales (II, i, 114-6) is merely a slighting reference to an out-of-date source of humour.

There is really no evidence that Rastell was himself the compiler, though the ponderous wit and diffuse prose do at least allow the possibility. Certainly, he was writing a lot in the 1520s and shifting his attention away from legal education towards humanist elegance and moral teaching. P.M. Zall, the book's most recent editor, notes:

> Many of its jests are patently intended to familiarize the 'unlearned' with such mysteries as the Pater Noster, the Creed, the Ave Maria, and the Seven Deadly Sins. Others are just as patently directed at teaching the newly 'civilized' Welsh the rudiments of urban gentility. And, fundamentally, the majority of the jests illuminate the superiority of common sense over wittol-like logic-chopping or scholastic dogmatizing.

This may be something of an overstatement; Tudor wits laughed at the Welsh and Irish without any concern for improving their social graces, and ridicule of the ignorant and the overly precise both was and is pretty universal.

Jest Number 7 of this edition—9 in the second version—is repeated from the *Interlude of the Four Elements*.

This book is the first I know of to identify the Cheapside house by the sign of the Mermaid, and the last to contain the large device without border damage. It marks also the first appearance of the 220 textura.

Copies of "C talis" appeared in Rastell's post-mortem inventory (Roberts 4). Since the numerals of the inventory apparently refer to the count of the copies, two hundred copies, the evaluation gives a price of a penny a copy, at least in 1538.

16   *Old Tenures*

Anonymous, *The Tennris*. Law French with English translation by John Rastell. c.1525. 2°. Reprinted from his edition of c.1521 (13).

No title; text begins on A1 under heading "T[lombardic cap]he T[lombardic cap]ennris" followed by row of type ornaments 6x43.

Colophon: **Impreſſum cum priuilegio*

Collation: 2°, A^6 B^4, 10 unnumbered leaves; $3 (-B3, +A1) signed textura.

Contents: A1: heading | text in two columns. left Law French, right English, each beginning with a two-line lombardic capital **T**, after which sections begin with paragraph marks, to B4: left column "¶**Finis.**" | centred colophon. B4^v: [within a frame of ornamental strips, left 3, upper 8, right 6, lower 2, device McKerrow 37].

Type: text (B2) 40 11., 187 (191) x 133; Law French column 186x51; English column 187x76; Law French 94 bastard, English 93a textura, heading and colophon 116 textura.

Examined: Harvard Beale T71.

Notes: STC 23880.3; Beale T71; bound with the *Terms* (17) and probably issued as a set with them.

The post-mortem inventory listed 124 "old tenures english and french," containing one ream of paper (Roberts 14).

17   *Terms*

John Rastell, *Exposiciones Terminorum Legum Anglorum*. Law French and English, preface by Rastell. c.1525. 2°. Reprinted from 14, *q.v.* for information on later printings.

No title; text begins on A1 under paragraph headings as follows: Latin title: "E[lombardic cap²]Xpoſiciones ſmnior' legū anglor'. Et | natura breuium cū diuerſes caſibus re | gulis & fundamentis legum tam de libris | Magiſtri Litteltoni quam de aliis legum | libris collectis & breuiter compilatis ꝑ Iu | uinibȝ valde neceſſariis'. | T[lombardic cap²]He expoſicions of the termys of ẙ law of englond | & the nature of the wryttys wyth dyuers rulis and | prīcyples of yᵉ law | aſwell out of ẙ bokys of maſter lyttel | ton as of other bokys of the law gaderid & breuely cōpilid | for yong men very neceſſary.' .'"

Colophon: ¶Impryntyd at Lodō ī chepe | ſyde at powlys gate.'. | C[lombardic cap]um priuilegio regali.'.

Collation: A⁸ B-F⁶ G⁴, 42 unnumbered leaves; $3 (-G3, +A4) signed [textura].

Contents: A1: title and table in three columns to A1ᵛ. A2: row of type ornaments 6x24 **Prologus Iohannis Raſtell.**" [row of type ornaments 6x35] | "L[text cap⁵]ykewiſe as ..." to A2ᵛ. A3: text in two columns, left Law French and right English, to G4: explicit under Law French column, "¶Adeſt huius libri finis pro | tempore preſenti.'."; explicit under English column, "¶Thus endyth thys boke for | thys preſent tyme.'. | [within a frame of ornamental strips, left 5, right 7, device McKerrow 37] | colophon. G4ᵛ: [within a frame of ornamental strips, left 6, upper 2, right 5, left 3, device McKerrow 37]

Type: text (A2) 40 11., 187 (193) x 130; Law French column 187x51; English 187x75; Law French 94 bastard, English 93a textura, headings, first line of preface, and first line of English 116 textura.

Examined: Harvard Beale T452.

Notes: STC 20703.3; Beale T452; Cowley 20. The copy is bound with the *Old Tenures* (16).

18   Littleton, *Tenures*

Sir Thomas Littleton, *Tenures*. Possibly translated by John Rastell. c.1525. 2°. Reprinted by Peter Treveris for Rastell c.1525 (19); by Thomas Berthelet in 1538 (STC 15761), and again in 1539 (STC 15761.6) and 1545 (STC 15764.5); by Robert Redman c.1539 (STC 15761.4) and c.1540 (STC 15761.8); by Robert Pettel in c.1541 (STC 15762); by William Middleton in 1544 (STC 15463); by William Powell in 1548 (STC 15765) and 1551 (15765.5); then by Richard Tottell, to whom the copy passed (Arber II.419) in 1556, who did thirteen editions to 1593, and finally became part of the Stock of the Stationers' Company, after passing through the hands of Charles Yetswiert, common law text patentee, who did editions in 1594 and 1597 (STC 15775 and 15776). See STC 15759.5 to 15783, and Beale T39-T61.

Title: **Lyttelton tenures in Englysshe,**

Collation: 2°, A-I^6 K-L^4, 62 leaves foliated.

Type: (fragment of fol. 30) 196 (204) x 140, 93a textura.

Examined: British Library Nash Fragment, two leaves, the first foliated "**.xxx.**"; further information from Raphel King Catalogue 46 (1947), item 185, still untraced.

Notes: STC 15759.5. Evidently it contained the usual device, McKerrow 37, and probably the same ornamental strips as those in 19.

There is no evidence to show that Rastell was the translator of this important book, but the facts that he was writing much in the 1520's and that he was greatly concerned with publishing clear texts in legal education allow for the possibility. Certainly this seems the first English text of Littleton's *Tenures*, which had been current in French since the previous century and has indeed been described as being in the French text "the earliest treatise on the English law printed anywhere."

19   Littleton, *Tenures*

Sir Thomas Littleton, *Tenures*. Possibly translated by John Rastell. c.1525. 2°. Reprinted by Peter Treveris for Rastell from 18.

Title: [within a frame of ornamental strips below two woodcuts of the 23x23 series, left 8, upper 7, right 14, lower 6: two woodcuts of the 23x23 series] | ¶**Lyttelton tenures** | **in Englyſſhe** | [two woodcuts of the 23x23 series]

Collation: 2°, A-I^6 K^8, 62 leaves foliated [1] **i-vii ix ix-xi xi-xiii xiii xv-xxvi xxviii xxviiii xxix-liiii liiii lvi-lix lx** (=62); $3 signed [textura].

RT [follows text with **Fo.**]

Contents: A1: title. A1^V: "¶**The Table.**". A2 "**Fee ſimple.**" [RT used as sub-heading] | **T**[init^7 33x32]**Enant ...**", text under nine headings, each beginning text cap^3 to B2^V: "¶**Thus endeth the fyrſt boke.** | ¶**The ſec-onde boke.** | **H**[init^8 36x36]**Omage...**", text under twelve headings as above to D3^V: "¶**The thyrde boke.** | **P**[lombardic cap^2]**Ercerers...**", text under twelve headings to K7: "**F I N I S.**". K7^V: "¶**Here begynneth the table** | **of this preſent boke.** | **N**[text cap^2]**Ow...**", contents of books. K8: blank. K8^V: [within a frame of ornamental strips left 14, upper 8, right 7, lower 6, device McKerrow 37] | "**Cum priuilegio.**".

CW] A-B **And** B-C **In the** C-D **[with] out lycence** D-E **caſe the [the leſſee]** E-F **any of [ony of]** F-G **for this** G-H **the dyſſeyly [the dyſieyly]** H-I **for the** I-K **and the**

Type: text (A5) 45 11., 208 (219) x 141, 93b textura, RT and first line of first and second books 116 textura, title and heading of second book 220 textura.

Examined: British Library C.54.k.9.

Notes: STC 15760; Beale T71; Dibdin 858; University Microfilms 12. This is the first book printed for Rastell by Peter Treveris in Southwark, using the 92b type which is almost identical to Rastell's, and in this book using his ornaments as well.

Rastell seems not to have reprinted this text after the two consecutive editions, and indeed there were 430 "littiltons in english" containing 23½ reams of paper in his shop at the post-mortem inventory (Roberts 8). Thomas Berthelet reprinted it in 1538, after which it seems to have been kept in print with new editions at intervals. The modern edition is by Eugene Wambaugh (Washington, D.C., 1903).

20   *The Widow Edith*

Walter Smith, *The wydow Edyth*. 23 March 1525 [i.e. 1525?]. Reprinted by W. Williamson? for R. Johnes, 1576 (STC 22807).

Colophon: **¶Thus endyth the boke of the lyeng | wydow Edyth. Enprynted at London at | the ſygne of ẏ Meremayd at Poliſ | gate next to Chepeſyde | The | yere of our Lord | M.v.C.xxv. ¶The | .xxiij. day of | March.**

Collation: 2°, a-c⁶ d⁴, 22 unnumbered leaves; $3 signed [textura].

RT] **The preface; The furſt** [to] **twelfth** [without error or variation] **geſt**

Contents: al: [within a frame of ornamental strips, left justified by woodcut of the 23x14 series, right woodcut of the 23x14 series justifying ornamental strip] **T**[lombardic cap]**He wydow Edyth** | [woodcut 23x14] | [ornamental strip] | **.xii. mery geſtys of one callyd Edyth | The lyeng wydow whych yet ſtyll lyueth** | **T**[lombardic cap²]**His** ...", text to middle of page: "**The preface** | **I**[text cap²]**N**...", text to a2: "**The furſt geſt** | **T**[lombardic cap²]**Homas Ellys** ...", text under twelve headings, each beginning lombardic cap², to d4: "**¶Quod walterus Smyth.**" | [within a frame of ornamental strips, left 10, upper 11, right 13, lower 12, 130x101 enclosing 107x73 device McKerrow 37] | "**C**[lombardic cap]**um priuilegio | Regali.**". d4ᵛ: [within a frame of ornamental strips, left 8, no upper, right 5, lower 12, 151x94 enclosing 136x73 device McKerrow 37].

Type: text (b1) 44 11., 204 (215) x 103, 93a textura, title, headings, running titles, explicit, first line of colophon, and privilege 116 textura.

Examined: The late Earl Fitzwilliam's copy, once on deposit at Magdalene College, Cambridge, since removed by the family; fragments at British Library, Harleian 5995/189, 191, 193, and the Bodleian, Vet A.1.b.12.

Notes: STC 22869.7. This book is significant in the Rastell bibliography for several reasons. It appears to be the first book in which the shop at Paul's Gate is identified as the Sign of the Mermaid; it is the first dated book to contain device McKerrow 37 with the base and top margin breaks that seem to have occurred in 1525. Also, it would appear to mark the beginning of an extensive series of books of humanist and educational concerns, closely related to the family and friends of More, whose servant Walter Smith was and in whose house the tricks of the widow were perpetrated. These books are mostly without date, but probably were all printed between 1525 and 1527 or 1528, when Rastell again began using his press for legal works of public importance.

The post-mortem inventory included 117 copies of this book or a later edition, containing three reams of paper (Roberts 22). While there is no evidence of an edition between this one and that of 1576, the printer Robert Copland has indicated that it was a popular work, when a customer in one of his prefaces asks:

> Hast thou a boke of the wydowe Edith
> That hath begyled so many with her wordes,
> Or els suche a geest that is ful of bourdes?
> Let me se; I wyll yet waste a peny
> Upon suche thynges and if thou have eny.

W.C. Hazlitt edited the text of the 1576 edition in *Shakespeare Jest-Books,* 3 (London, 1864), pp. 30-108.

21   Lucian, *Necromantia*

Lucian of Samosata, *Necromantia*. Translated into Latin by Thomas More and into English verse possibly by Rastell. Printed for Rastell by Peter Treveris. *2°*. c.1523-1526.

Title: [within a frame of ornamental strips from Treveris's shop 205x152 enclosing 154x130] **¶Necromantia, | ¶A dialog of the Poete Lucyan for his fanteſye faynyd | for a mery paſtyme. And furſt by hym copylyd in the | greke tonge. And after tranſlated owt of greke | in to latyn | and now latly tranſlatyd owt | of laten in to englyſſh" for the erudicio | of them which be diſpoſyd to | lerne the tongis. | ¶**Interlocutores. Menippus et Philonides. | [ornamental strip 20x127] | [woodcut of royal arms 70x78]

Colophon: **¶Iohannes Raſtell me fieri fecit. | ¶Cum priuilegio regali.**

Collation: 2°, A⁶ B⁴, 10 unnumbered leaves; $3 (-B3) signed [roman with roman numerals].

Contents: A1: title (verso blank). A2ᵃ. "**¶Menippus. | Exam. O**[lombardic cap²]**Thou ...**". A2ᵇ: MENIPPVS. | S[cap²]Alue ...": text in two columns, English in inner and Latin in outer, to B4. On B4ᵃ: "**¶Finis.**". On B4ᵇ: "**¶Necromantiae ſeu Menippi Lu | ciani Finis.**". B4ᵛ: [within a frame of ornamental strips from Treveris's stock, device McKerrow 37].

Type: text (B1) 42 11., 196 (200) x 143; English column 196x82; Latin column 192x52; English 93b textura; Latin 94 roman, first line of title 220 textura, remainder and colophon 116 textura.

Examined: Bodleian Douce fragm. f.13; while the location of the complete copy is well known, I have had to guarantee not to say where it is in this study. [According to the most recent *STC*, the copy belongs to the Earl of Macclesfield.]

Notes: STC 16895; University Microfilms 965. The post-mortem inventory included 500 copies containing "vij remis" of paper (Roberts 9). A hundred copies remained at the Sign of the Sun, to which they had presumably been brought by Wynkyn de Worde or John Byddell, as late as 1553. See H.H. Plomer, "An Inventory of Wynkyn de Worde's House 'The Sun in Fleet Street' in 1553," *The Library*, 3rd ser. 6 (1915), pp. 228-34.

Like the other humanist books of this period of Rastell's life, this book is obviously connected with the friends of Thomas More. The Latin text of the dialogue is that of More's translation from the Greek, first published with Erasmus's translations of 1506. C.R. Thompson suggests Rastell as the English translator, in *Translations of Lucian, Complete Works of St. Thomas More*, iii (New Haven and London, 1974), p. 142. It is indeed possible that, during these few years of cultivated leisure when he even had time to stage moral plays on his own stage, and, given his other efforts to promote English culture, Rastell did translate the text. However, both the cadences and the diction seem a bit too good for Rastell, by comparison with his other writing in English verse:

> Me thought ma*n*nys lyfe wel be lykenid might
> To a stage play where it fortunyth alway
> That they that be the players shalbe *tha*t day
> Apparelyd in dyuers strau*n*ge clothyng
> As rych aray for hym that playeth the king
> With a purpyll cap & a crown of gold theron ...

If my dating, based solely on topic, format, and the state of the larger printer's device, is correct, then this text also marks the first use by Rastell of "fieri fecit" or "imprimi fecit," a form of explicit or ending statement he used only a few times. Both Greg and Reed felt that it implied authorship as well as the printing of the texts, which may indeed be true, but this conclusion seems to me by no means certain. The phrase is in fact a playful variation of the legal phrase "Fieri facias," the name of the writ ordering a sheriff to seize and sell the goods of a debtor, and I imagine a personal joke about the various financial difficulties Rastell was experiencing at the time, especially over the building of his house and stage, which were matters for a future lawsuit.

22   *Calisto and Melebea*

Anonymous, *A new commodye in englysh* [The interlude of Calisto and Melebea]. c.1525-1527. 2°.

Title: **A** [lombardic cap² to left of text, not dropped into it]**new c̄omodye in englyſh in maner | Of an enterlude ryght elygant & full of craft | of rethoryk | wherin is ſhewd & dyſcrybyd as | well the bewte & good propertes of women/ | as theyr vycys & euyll c̄odic̄os/ with a morall | c̄ocluſion & exhortacyon to vertew**

Colophon: **Iohēs raſtell me imprimi fecit | Cum priuilegio regali**

Collation: 2°, A⁶ B-C⁴, 14 unnumbered leaves; $2 (+A1, 3) signed [textura].

Contents: A1: title | ornamental strip 11 | ornamental strip 13 | "**Melebea | ¶ Franciſcus ...**", text with speaker's names in full at first and then usually, though not always, abbreviated to an initial or "**Ca**", in left margins on each page, to C3ᵛ: "**Amen**" | colophon. C4: [within a frame of ornamental strips, left 14, upper 13 right 12, lower 10, twelve woodcuts of the 23x23 series, in three rows of four]. C4ᵛ: [within a frame of ornamental strips, left 12, upper 10, right 14, lower 13 device McKerrow 37].

Type: text (A6) 44 11., 205 (209) x 91; 93a textura with small capital H throughout; first line of title, first heading, and privilege 116 textura; a stage direction on C2 is in 84 bastard.

Examined: Bodleian Malone 22, with part of line 42 on A5 cut out by a reader. It is impossible to tell whether the offending passage was on A5, where the text apparently identified a "frere" who was a substantial "lode" for a woman, or on A5ᵛ, where the servant Parmeno was describing "an old hore."

Notes: STC 20721; Dibdin 853; Greg 10; University Microfilms 1286. The text was issued in facsimile by John S. Farmer, Tudor Facsimile Texts (London and Edinburgh, 1909, repr. New York, 1970); it was edited by W.W. Greg, Malone Society (Oxford, 1908); by H.W. Allen (London, 1908); and by Richard Axton in *Three Rastell Plays* (Cambridge, 1979), intro. pp. 15-20, text pp. 69-96, and notes pp. 140-52.

The colophon form is another variation of the "fieri facias" writ title. Greg felt that it might have implied authorship as well as publication of the interlude, as did Reed in *Early Tudor Drama*. C.R. Baskervill noted in "John Rastell's Dramatic Activities," *Modern Philology* 13 (1916), p. 558, that the didactic moralizing of the interlude, with Melebea's refusal to fall into sin, suited Rastell's main concerns. But they suited those of his friends as well, and there is little in the style of the interlude to suggest Rastell, except perhaps at the end.

The interlude is based on *La Celestina*, Fernando de Rojas' dialogue novel of 1499, but omits a great deal from its Spanish original to produce a simple morality play. Indeed, the English writer has even left out Melebea's suicide and provided a happy ending in which, with her virtue intact, she repents having even come near sin, because she has been well brought up to virtue. In the true Rastell manner, it is argued that a world in which the young will be so brought up must be governed by good laws, which should prevent evil rather than merely punish. These are combined into a final assertion that the young must learn trades and how to work, for the good of their souls as well as their well-being in the world.

The final exhortation, as Axton so nicely puts it, has "all John Rastell's familiar hobby-horses ... trotted out;" its message is close to that of the *Utopia*, and is reinforced by the characterization of Calisto as a fashion-able lover and user of Petrarchan love language, a useless person who would have no place in Rastell's ideal world. The adaptation has been been effectively studied by Axton and by H.D. Purcell in "The *Celestina* and the *Interlude of Calisto and Melibea*," *Bulletin of Hispanic Studies* 44 (1967), pp. 1-15.

Rastell's post-mortem inventory listed 370 copies containing five reams of paper (Roberts 11).

23   *Gentleness and Nobility*

Anonymous [John Heywood and/or John Rastell], *Of Gentylnes & Noby-lyte*. c.1525-1527. 2°.

Title: [not centred] ⟨¶ **Of Gen | tylnes & Nobylyte | A dyaloge betwen the marchaut the | Knyght & the plowman dyſputyng who is a verey | gentylman & who is a noble man and how men | ſhuld | come to auc-toryte | compilid in maner of an | enterlude with diuers toys & geſtis addyd therto | to make mery paſtyme and diſport. | ⅋**

Colophon: **Iohes raſtell me fieri fecit | Cum priuilegio regali.**

Collation: 2°, A^6, B-C^4, 14 unnumbered leaves; $3 signed [textura]

Contents: A1:title | "**The marchaunt | O[cap^3] what...**", text to A6^V: "**Amen | Finis prime partis | Secunda pars | The Plouman | Here ...**", text to C3^V: "**Amen | The phyloſopher | ye ...** ", text to C4^V: "**A M E N. | colophon | ornamental strip 2 | ornamental strip 12**

Type: text (A3) 44 11., 204 (210) x 87; 93a textura with small capital H, first two lines of title and first person heading 116 textura.

Examined: Bodleian Ashm. 1766 (7), wanting A2.5 and with A3 mis-printed as A2; British Library C.40.i.16, wanting A1.6, C2.3; C.40.m.9/19 frag., A3.4 only; Nash fragment, A3.4, B1.4, B2.3, C1.4, C2.3 only; Cambridge Syn. 4.52.9; Cambridge, Pepys 1977.

Notes: STC 20723; Dibdin 855; Greg 8, 9, 1 & 2; University Microfilms 140. The text was issued in facsimile by John S. Farmer, Tudor Facsimile Texts (London and Edinburgh, 1909, repr. New York, 1970); it was edited by K.W. Cameron in *Authorship and Sources of 'Gentleness and Nobility'* (Durham, N.C., 1941); by A.C. Partridge and F.P. Wilson, Mal-one Society (Oxford, 1950); and by Richard Axton in *Three Rastell Plays* (Cambridge, 1979), intro. pp. 20-26, text pp. 97-124, and notes pp. 153-60.

Eighty copies containing one ream of paper remained at the post-mortem inventory (Roberts 16).

The three characters are identified at their first speeches by headings occupying a line within the text, after which they appear in the left mar-gins, in all but three cases as initials M, K, or P. The heading on C3^V is for the Philosopher's Epilogue, yet another affirmation of all Rastell's ideas on making the world a better place.

There is naturally a question about the authorship of the interlude, with some tendency to see Rastell as the actual writer. C.R. Baskervill in

"John Rastell's Dramatic Activities," *Modern Philology*, 13 (1916), pp. 557-560, Esther C. Dunn in "John Rastell and 'Gentleness and Nobility,'" *Modern Language Review* 12 (1917), pp. 266-278, and A.W. Reed in *Early Tudor Drama* (London, 1926) all note that the theme of real as distinct from inherited nobility suited Rastell's concerns; but it could be replied that everything he published did. C. Tucker Brooke, on the other hand, argues in "*Gentleness and Nobility*: the Authorship and Source," *Modern Language Review* 6 (1911), pp. 458-461, that there were only two possible translations of "me fieri fecit," and that either could be seen as "a virtual disclaimer of Rastell's authorship;" this seems not all that self-evident, since the play on the writ title does in fact give the phrase a third meaning. Kenneth W. Cameron concluded in *Authorship and Sources of 'Gentleness and Nobility'* (Raleigh, North Carolina, 1941) that the interlude itself was probably written by John Heywood, Rastell's son-in-law, but that the epilogue spoken by the Philosopher, an extensive treatment of Rastell's normal concerns with the nature of nobility, the use of "naturall reason," and the need for good laws, was most likely Rastell's own addition, a weighty passage in rhyme royal standing out from the fast-paced couplets of the interlude text. Axton, in his excellent discussion of the interlude, agreed with Cameron, and though, as David Bevington wrote in *Tudor Drama and Politics* (Cambridge, Massachusetts, 1968), pp. 76-82, the question of authorship "can scarcely be resolved by the language itself," it seems certain enough that both these successive dramatic publications were written by friends of Rastell, both had moral and didactic purposes, and both had epilogues by the printer and owner of the stage himself.

24

Anonymous, "the abces with sillables." c.1525-1527. Nothing known of size or format, but probably a small quarto, especially if it was, as Roberts has suggested, an early edition of STC 19.4 and 19.5 (Roberts 17). Ninety copies remained at the Mermaid at the post-mortem inventory.

25   "A wey mornynge"

Anonymous, "A wey mornynge." c.1525-1527. 1°.

Text: fragmentary, music and three quatrains from conventional song against a false lady, with device McKerrow 40.

Type: Rastell's music type and 93a textura.

Examined: British Library K.8.k.8. fragment.

Notes: STC 20700.3; University Microfilms 1824. This is the first Rastell printing since the *Terms* (14) of c.1521 to use the smaller's printer's device McKerrow 40, which is more worn in the left margins than before and quite weak above.

The music type has been discussed above; it was first used in the *Interlude of the Four Elements* in about 1520 (12), and was later used by John Gough in printing Myles Coverdale's *Goostly psalmes* (STC 5892), ten copies of which were included in the post-mortem inventory of the shop (Roberts 19). The broadside has been studied so well by A. Hyatt King in "The Significance of John Rastell in Early Music Printing," *The Library*, 5th ser. 26 (1971), pp. 197-214 that nothing needs to be added to his consideration of the dating and printing of the broadside, except perhaps that the song is part of a very considerable body of publications in the middle of the decade expressive of cultivated leisure.

26   *Book of the New Cards*

Anonymous, John Rastell?, *The boke of the new cardys.* c.1525-1527. 4°.

Title: ¶T[lombardic cap]**he boke of the new cardys wh | pleyeng at cardſ one may lerne to know hys lett | ſpell & to rede & how one ſhuld wryte englyſh trew | to rede all nōbers as well comī nōbers as algori | And alſo to lerne to caſt accompt as well ye c̄ | countys as algoryſme wyth dyuers [o]yer prop | encys and c̄ocluſyons as here after in yis boke | ſpecyally ſhalbe declaryd**

Collation: 4°, a^6 [?] textura.

Contents: al: title | beginning of table, which indicates that the text went to at least nineteen chapters. Type: text (a6^v) 31 11., 141 x 94; 93a textura, first line of title 116 textura.

Examined: British Library Nash fragment, half-sheet quarto containing two impressions of a1 and what seems to be a6, the outer half sheet, then, for a gathering of quarto in sixes. Whether the whole book was quarto in sixes, like Rastell's earliest small books, or whether it was only the first gathering, as in the two small folios above, 22 and 23, cannot be ascertained from the fragment.

Notes: STC 3356.3; Ray Nash, "Rastell Fragments at Dartmouth," *The Library*, 4th series, 24 (1944), pp. 66-73, item 4. The dating is naturally based on the period in Rastell's career—between 1524, when he obviously began a time of humanist activity with plays and amusing or educational books, and 1527-1528, when he began to concentrate on more serious matters.

The Book of the New Cards was clearly intented as an educational experiment, a book to allow mature people to develop skills they had never learned in school. It was sold with a corresponding pack of cards, each card having "a dyuers letter in the myddys" and other letters in the borders. The package seems to demonstrate a devotion to uniformity in spelling uncommon at the time; the difference between e and o in single and double uses was treated, as well as rules governing the use of e at the ends of words "to perfor*me* *th*e sown." The identification and uses of both roman and arabic numerals follow, after which there are card games "wherby ye shall lerne to [kno]w your letters," "to tech *th*e pleyers to spell and [rea]de sillabuls or wordys," "to tech folke to cast accoun*tes*," and "to rede all no*m*[bers] of algorysme."

There is also special treatment of a th letter, described by Issac as a tail-less y, and of the fairly rare letter w. The th letter was presumably cut and cast for the book, and does not fit into the 93a textura fount very well; nor for that matter did the w that Rastell had added to the fount when he first acquired it. It would seem that this new letter, which was only ever used again in Rastell's *Pastime of People*, on A2, was originally intended to represent *th* wherever it might occur, unlike the familiar y, which was always used initially. Or at least so I read the title's reference to "o*th*er;" in the *Pastime* the letter is used only at the beginning of words.

27   Chaucer, *Parliament of Fowls*

Geoffrey Chaucer, *Here begynneth the parlyament of fowles*. Probably edited by and with a verse preface by John Rastell. c.1525-1527. 4° [in sixes?].

Title: ¶**Here begynneth the parlyamēt of | fowles compyled by the noble retho= | rycyen Geffray chaucer.**

Collation: 4°, a⁶[?]; a1 signed [textura].

Contents: a1: title | "¶**Iohānes Raſtell in laudem magiſtri gal= | fridi chaucer.**" | [woodcut Hodnett 2286] | w[small text cap³]Ho...", verse preface in rhyme royal to a1ᵛ. Text presumably begins at a2. The other surviving leaf, a2, is no longer conjugate with a1; it has 11. 225-280 of the text, which is correct for the ninth page.

Type: (a1) 152 (156) x 96; 93a textura, heading 116 textura. The main text has four stanzas of rhyme royal with spaces between them on each page.

Examined: Bodleian Douce fragments e.38, a1.6 only.

Notes: STC 5091.5. The woodcut, Hodnett 2286, was presumably made for this book; it was used again c.1540 in an edition of *The boke of hawkynge* (STC 3310) by Henry Tab, who seems to have been an employee of Rastell's and was one of the assessors of the post-mortem inventory. The inventory does not list copies of this book among items printed by Rastell, but among other books includes "a bok parte of Chaucer's workes" (Roberts 31).

Rastell's work in finding and editing the text and his enthusiastic preface in rhyme royal clearly set this book into the 1525 to 1527 period. If he found the text, as he says, "with oft inquisicyon" and "hyt publisshide & made to be prentyd," then his edition may be considered earlier than that of Richard Pynson (STC 5088 of c.1526) and that of Wynkyn de Worde (STC 5030). In the verse preface he takes up another of his old topics, the praise of the English language and those who help perfect it. For Rastell, Chaucer is seen as improving "our tonge":

> His hye sentence so brefe and quyke
> His pregnaunt resons of perfyte sustenaunce
> His sugred termys ar no thing to seke
> His collours gay of moste perfyte plesaunce
> So clere is depuryd his langage in substance

Of euery difference in his owne properte
Worde reson sentence poyntyd as it sholde be.

The text Rastell has edited or had edited seems to have little relation to that of the much earlier William Caxton edition (STC 5091), but seems related to that used by Pynson, whose text shares Rastell's reading of 1.225 as "Than sawe I beaute with a nyce atyre." The textual tradition was discussed some time ago by Eleanor Prescott Hammond in "On the Text of Chaucer's *Parliament of Foules*," *Decentennial Publications of the University of Chicago*, 1st ser. 7 (1903), pp. 1-25 and John Koch, *Geoffrey Chaucers Kleinere Dichtungen* (Heidelberg, 1928), neither of which treats the Rastell fragment, although its variations from the accepted textual tradition are unimportant. They are discussed in my "John Rastell's Text of *The Parliament of Fowls*," *Moreana* 27|28 (1970), pp. 115-120.

28   *Life of St Thomas a Becket*

Anonymous, *Life of St. Thomas a Becket.* c.1525-1527. 4°.

Colophon: ¶**Imprented in chepe ſyde next to Paulis gate**

Collation: 4°, nothing else known.

Contents: nothing known until last gathering, but clearly containing a life of Becket in rhyme royal, with each stanza beginning with a paragraph mark, but no space between stanzas. Last text page: text | colophon | "¶**Cum priuilegio regali.**" | [device McKerrow 40]; verso blank.

Type: text 31 11., 144 x 103; 93a textura, privilege 116 textura.

Examined: British Library Nash fragment.

Notes: STC 23954.3, dated 1520. The book, however, seems to me closer in time to the series of small books of humanist and moral concerns that appeared between 1525 and roughly the beginning of 1528, when Rastell again devoted his press to more serious matters of concern.

While such an instinctive view cannot be called exact dating, it is noteworthy that eighty copies remained at the post-mortem inventory (Roberts 18), in which most books seem considerably later than 1520.

29   Skelton, *Against a comely Coystrowne*

John Skelton, *Agaynste a comely Coystrowne.* c. 1525-1527. 4°.

Title: S[lombardic cap]**kelton Laureate agaynſte a comely** | **Coyſtrowne that curyowſly chawntyd And curryſhly** | **cowntred"** **And madly in hys Muſyakys mokkyſhly** | **made** | **Agaynſte the .ix.** **Muſys of polytyke Poems &** | **Poettys matryculat.** | [within a frame of ornamental strips, left 3, upper 13, right 4, lower 11 woodcut Hodnett 2287]

Collation: 4°, A^4, 4 unnumbered leaves.

Contents: A1: title. A1^v: "o[lower case text cap^3]F ... ", text to A4^v: "C[lombardic cap]**um priuilegio**]

Type: text (A3) 31 11., 146 x 93; 93a textura, first line of title and privilege 116 textura.

Examined: Huntington 59200.

Notes: STC 22611; University Microfilms 860. This book and the following one, *Dyuers Balettys,* have been fully treated by Robert S. Kinsman in "The Printer and Date of Publication of Skelton's *Agaynste a Comely Coystrowne* and *Dyuers Balettys,*" *Huntington Library Quarterly* 16 (1953), pp. 203-210. Kinsman attributes both books to Rastell's press on typographical evidence, the use of 93a textura.

30   Skelton, *Diverse Ballads*

John Skelton, *Here Folowythe dyuers Balletys and dyties.* c.1525-1527.
4°.

Title: [within a frame of ornamental strips, left 6, upper type ornaments,
right 9, lower 11], **H**[lombardic cap^2]**E**[lombardic cap]**re Folowythe
dyuers | Balettys and dyties ſola= | cyous deuyſyd by Maſter Skel= |
ton Laureat.** [row of type ornaments] | [row of type ornaments] | [wood-
cut Hodnett 2287]

Contents: *A*1: title. *A*1^V: "⸿ **with lullay lullay** ...", text of group of poems
to *A*4^V. On A2: within a frame, left a cut of the 24x13 series, upper ornamental strip 4, right cut of the 24x13 series, lower ornamental strip 12
"**Qd** | **Skelton** | **Laureate.** ⸫". On *A*4: ornamental strip 13. On *A*4^V:
"**C**[lombardic cap]**um priuilegio.**".

Type: text (*A*3) 31 11., 146 x 93; 93a textura, title and privilege 116 textura.

Examined: Huntington 59201.

Notes: STC 22604; University Microfilms 860; Kinsman, 203-210. The
text contains five poems, none of them new.

31   Skelton, *Philip Sparrow*

John Skelton, *Philip Sparrow*. c.1525-1527. 4° (?). Reprinted by Robert Copland for Richard Kele, 1545? or slightly earlier, in octavo (reprinted version is STC 22594; University Microfilms 1642).

Notes: Roberts 12, listing 213 copies totalling three reams. If, as seems likely, this matched the previous two printings of early Skelton poetry, then it probably collated A-G^4 or A-C^6 D^4, with 31 lines to a page, woodcut Hodnett 2287 on the title page, and no address in the colophon.

32   Skelton, *Ware the Hawk*

John Skelton, *Ware the Hawk*. c.1525-1527. 4° (?).

Notes: The post-mortem inventory gives no indication of the size of the book, but lists 28 copies, which with four other books total one ream of paper (Roberts 20). If it had the usual 31 lines to a page, its 337 lines and ten headings would likely appear as a quarto with two gatherings.

There was no other separate edition of the poem.

33   *Accidentia*

John Stanbridge, *Accidentia*. 4° in sixes. c.1525-1527. Partly printed for Rastell by Peter Treveris. Earlier editions by Pynson and de Worde and some continental printers (STC 23139.5 to 23148.7, 16 editions in all), and later editions by de Worde and others (STC 23148.10 to 23152, 15 editions in all).

Title: **Accidentia ex ſtanbrigiana | editione** | [row of four chevron type ornaments] | [ornamental strip 3] | [woodcut Hodnett 2289]

Colophon: **¶Impryntyd in chepe ſyde at the ſyne of the | meare mayd next to pollys gate.**

Collation: 4°, A-B⁶ C4, 16 unnumbered leaves; $3 (-C3) signed [textura].

No RT or CW, but **Stam. accidence.** occurs on AC2, A3 and *Acci.* ſtan. on B1-3 in direction lines.

Contents A1: title. A1ᵛ: [woodcut Hodnett 2289]. A2: "H[text cap⁴]owe ...", text in six sections, each beginning with lombardic cap², to C4ᵛ: colophon.

Type: text (A3) 33 11., 154 (158) x 99; 93a textura in $AC, 93b textura in $B, title 116 textura.

Examined: Bodleian Tanner 239 (1).

Notes: STC 23148.8, formerly 23145; Dibdin 856. Treveris printed a later edition under his own imprint (STC 23149.5).

34   *Terms*

John Rastell, *Exposiciones terminorum legum anglorum.* Law French and English, preface by Rastell. c.1525-1527. 2°. Reprinted from his earlier editions (see 14 for details of later printings).

No title: text begins on A1 under paragraph headings as follows: Latin title: "**E**[lombardic cap²]**Xpoﬁciones ꝛminor' legū anglor'. Et | natura breuiū cū diuerﬁs caﬁbus re= | gulis & fundamentis legum tam de libris | Magiﬆri Litteltoni quam de aliis legum | libris collectis & breuiter compilatis p̄ Iu= | uinibᵹ valde neceﬄariis.**" | English title: "**T**[lombardic cap²]**He expoﬁcions of the termys of ẙ law of englond ı & the nature of the wryttys wyth dyuers rulys and pryncyples of yᵉ law | aﬀwell out of ẙ bokys of maﬆer lyttel= | ton as of other bokys of the law gaderyd & breuely cōpilyd | for yong men very neceﬄary.**"

Colophon: **¶Imprynted at Lōdō ī chepe | ﬁyde at powlys gate. | C**[lombardic cap]**um priuilegio regali.˙.**

Collation: 2°, A⁸ B-F⁶ G⁴, 42 unnumbered leaves; $3 (-AG3, +A4, misprinting A2 as A) signed [textura].

A1: headings and table in three columns to A1ᵛ. A2: [row of type ornament 6x23] "**P**[lombardic cap]**rologus Iohannis Raﬆell.**" [row of type ornament 6x32] | "**L**[cap⁵]**ykewiﬀe as ...**" to A2ᵛ. A3: text in two columns, left Law French and right English, each beginning with Lombardic cap A, ² for Law French, ³ for English, after which each entry begins with a paragraph mark, to G4: explicit under Law French column, "**¶Adeﬆ huius libri finis pro | tempora preﬀenti.**"; last line of English column | explicit: "**¶Thus endyth thys boke for | thys preﬀent tyme.˙.**" | [between ornamental strips, left 7, right 9, device McKerrow 37] | colophon. G4ᵛ:[within a frame of ornamental strips, left 13, upper 11, right 10, lower 12, 135x100 enclosing 107x72, device McKerrow 37].

Type: text (C1) approximately 40 ll., 191 (187) x 130; Law French column 187x51; English column 187x75; Law French 94 bastard, English 93a textura; headings, first line of preface, and first line of English text 116 textura.

Examined: British Library C.64.h.2.; Harvard Beale T452.

Notes: STC 20703; Beale T452; Cowley 20; Dibdin 836; University Microfilms 140.

35   *Hundred Merry Tales*

Anonymous, possibly John Rastell, *A, C, mery talys.* 22 November 1526. 2°. All but $B printed by Peter Treveris from a revised text of 15.

Title: [within a frame of ornamental strips, left 9, upper 13, right 5, lower 11, two woodcuts of the 23x23 series | ornamental strip 2] | **A, C, mery talys,** | [ornamental strip 3 | two woodcuts of the 23x23 series]

Colophon: ⸿**Thus endeth the booke of a. C. mery** | **talys. Empryntyd at London at the ſygne of** | **the Merymayd At Powlys gate next** | **to chepe ſyde.** ⸿**The yere** | **of our Lorde .M.v.C.xxvi.** ¶**The .xxii.** | **day of Noueber.**

Collation: 2°, A^4 B-E^6, 28 leaves foliated [1-2] **i xxvi iii-xxv xxi** (+28); $3 (-A3) signed [textura].

RT: Folio. [with number, on rectos]; Folios. B5.

Contents: A1: title. A1^v: "¶**The kalender**" | single column to A2^v: "**Finis.**". A3: "**A**[text cap^7]**Certayn Curat** ...", text under 100 headings, each beginning with paragraph marks [on C2 cap A is omitted], to D6: "¶**Finis.**". D6^v: colophon | [within a frame of three ornamental strips, all belonging to Treveris, device McKerrow 37] | "¶**Cum preuilegio** [stet] | **Kegali.**" [stet]

Type: Text (E3) 41 11., 191 (202) x 130, 93b textura except for $b, 93a textura, title 220 textura, first line of colophon and privilege 116 textura.

Examined: Niedersächsische Staats- und Universitätsbibliothek, Göttingen 4° Fab. Rom. IX, 150 Rara, originally from the Royal Library. For information I am grateful to Dr. Haenel.

Notes: STC 23664; University Microfilms 1397. As mentioned in the notes on 15, there seem to have been a hundred copies left at the post-mortem inventory (Roberts 4). There are considerable differences between 15 and this edition, and it has been suggested, most recently in the revised STC, that this might have been the earlier edition. The break in the base of the device, however, which is very clear in this edition, does not appear at all in 15, which must have been printed before 1525, when the damage seems to have occurred.

This later edition has been heavily revised. There is much variation and there are some changes in order.

The text has been edited by Herman Oesterly in *Shakespeare's Jest Book: A Hundred Merry Tales* (London, 1866) and more recently by P.M. Zall in *A Hundred Merry Tales and Other English Jestbooks of the Fifteenth and Sixteenth Centuries* (Lincoln, Nebraska, 1963).

36   *Terms*

John Rastell, *Expositiones Terminorum Legum Anglorum.* Law French text only, with English preface by Rastell. 15 July 1527. 16° in eights. Reprinted by Peter Treveris for Rastell from the earlier editions; see notes to 14.

Title: E[initial^5 23x15]xpoſitiones terminorū le= | gum anglorū. Et natura bre= | uium cum diuerſis caſibus re= | gulis & fundamentis legū tam | de libris Magiſtri Litteltoni | quā de alijs legum libris collectis | et breuiter compilatis pro | iuuinibus valde | neceſſarijs. | ∴

Colophon: Impreſſum .xv. die Iulij. anno dn̄i | M.v.C.xxvii. | Cum priuilegio regali.

Collation: 16°, +^{8}, A-N^8, 112 leaves foliated [1-8] i-ciii [104] (=112); $4 (N3, ++1) signed [bastard].

RT: **Folio.** with number, on rectos to D; from D **Fo.**, with the following exceptions: **Fo.** on B8, C2, 4, 6, 8, D1, N3, N5, N6; **Foli.** on N7, **Folio** C7.

Contents: =+1: title. =1^v: table in single column beginning "A[lombardic cap^3]Biuration ..." to +6^v. +7: "¶Prohemium. | L[lombardic cap^2]ykewyſe as ..." to +8^v: "AMEN.". A1: text beginning with lombardic cap A^2, with each entry with heading beginning with paragraph mark, to N7: "Finis" | colophon. N7^v: blank. N8: [woodcut Hodnett 2282]. N8^v: [woodcut Hodnett 2283].

Type: text (E2) 19 11., 80 (88) x 93, 81 bastard, first line of title and of prohemium 94 bastard.

Examined: British Library C.40.g.2.; Cambridge SSS.20.15 (with $C bound between M and N); Cambridge Syn. 8.52.22; Cambridge Syn. 8.52.43 (wanting part of N7, 8); Harvard Beale T453.

Notes: STC 20703; Beale T453; Cowley 10; Dibdin 863; University Microfilms 140.

37   *Book of the Justice of Peace*

The boke of the Iustyce of peas. c. 1527-1528. 8°. Reprinted from earlier editions of Richard Pynson and others, and frequently reprinted by others; see Beale T130-T157 and STC 14871-14887, several editions containing the whole series of legal tracts that here follow. Rastell presumably intended the books, 37 to 42 in this bibliography, to be sold individually or as a single volume.

Title: T[lombardic cap]**he boke of the Iuſtyce of | peas/ the charge with all the | proces of the ceſſyons neuly | correctyd and amendyd with | dyuers new addycyons put | to the ſame.|** [woodcut of Royal Arms 46x50, very battered with most of the border gone; similar but not identical to Beale No. 5]

Collation: 8°, a-k^8, 80 leaves unnumbered to f5^v, which is "Folio .i."; f6 is "Fo .ii.", then from f7 foliated iii-xxxiiii [35-38] (=80); $4 signed [rotunda].

RT: from gl^v **Fo.** or **Folio.** occurs on versos with the foliation on rectos.

Contents: al: title (verso blank); a2: "**w**[text size rotunda^5]**Hat** ...", text to k5: within last line: "**FINIS.**" k5^v: "**¶Tabula**", repeated in the manner of a running title but without the paragraph mark to k7; text of table to k7^v: "**FINIS.**".k8^{r-v}: blank.

Type: text (b4) 28 11., 93 (96) x 67; 67 rotunda; the title-page type may be Treveris's 120 textura.

Examined: Bodleian 8° I 22. Jur. (1); Harvard Beale T137.

Notes: STC 14871; Beale T137; Dibdin 859; University Microfilms 70. The Bodleian copy has a note by E.G. Duff, identifying the printer as Rastell and the date as c.1527.

38   *Carta Feodi*

Paruus libellus continens formam multarum rerum. c.1527-1528. 8°
Often called *Carta Feodi*. Reprinted from earlier editions by Pynson and
others, and frequently reprinted; see Beale T158-T179 and STC 15579.3
- 15587.5.

Title: missing in the two copies I have seen.

Collation: 8°, A-E^8 F^4, 44 leaves foliated [1] ii-xl [41-44]; $4 (-F2-4)
signed [rotunda].

RT: **Folio** on versos with the foliation on rectos.

Contents: A1: title (verso blank); A2: "**ii.** | **¶ Paruus libellus continens
formam multarū | rerum prout patet in kalendario in fine in ſtento.
| ¶Carta feodi ſimplices cum | littera atturnatoria.** | [woodcut of Royal
Arms 46x50, as described in 37, inset into text[14]] S[lombardic cap]**ciant**
...**"**; text to F2: "**Kalendarium huius libri**". F2^v: **Kalendarium huius
libelli.**, single column to F4^v.

Type: text (B1) 28 11., 93 (96) x 67; 67 rotunda.

Examined: Bodleian 8° I 22. Jur. (2); Harvard Beale T165.

Notes: STC 15581.2; Beale T165; Dibdin 859. As noted in 37 this is part
of a series of tracts issued together.

39   *Hundred Courts*

Modus tenendi vnum Hundredum. c.1527-1528. 8°. Reprinted from earlier editions by Pynson and others, and frequently reprinted; see Beale T202-T216 and STC 7725.9 - 77342.

Title:¶**Modus tenendi vnum Hundre=** | **du̅ ſiue curiam de Recordo.** | [woodcut of Royal Arms 46-50, as described in 37]

Collation: 8°, A-B^{8}C^4, 20 unnumbered leaves; $4 signed, misprinting A4 (E4), [rotunda].

Contents: A1: title. A1^v: [woodcut of Royal Arms as described in 37]. A2: "¶**Colceſtr.** | **H**[lombardic cap^3]**Vndredu̅ ...**", text to C3^v: "F I N I S". C4: blank. C4^v: [device McKerrow 37].

Type: text (B1) 28 11., 93 (96) x 67; 67 rotunda.

Examined: Bodleian 8° I 22. Jur. (3); Harvard Beale T205.

Notes: STC 7727; Beale T205; Dibdin 859; University Microfilms 78 and also 784. The new STC notes that it "Should collate A-B^8 C^{4,} with B1^r line 1 beginning 'w. B. vni', B6^r having additions beginning: 'En dette,' and Rastell's device, McK 37, w. his name on C4^v. All copies have instead B^8 belonging to 7712, 42 below in this bibliography. This Hundred Court text is reprinted in 18394 [William Rastell's edition of 1534]; the additions are incorporated in Court Baron in 7712.3 [Thomas Berthelet's edition of c.1533]."

40   *Returna Breuium*

Returna breuium. c.1527-1528. 8°. Reprinted from earlier editions by Pynson and others, and frequently reprinted; see Beale T217-T231 and STC 20894.4 -20904.

Title: **¶Returna breuium.** | ∴ | [woodcut of Royal Arms 46x50, as described in 37]

Collation: 8°, A^8 B^4, 12 unnumbered leaves; S4 (-B2-4) signed [rotunda].

Contents: A1: title (verso blank). A2: "**E**[lombardic cap^2]**N**...", text to B4^v: "**F I N I S.** ".

Type: text (B1) 28 11., 93 (96) x 67; 67 rotunda.

Examined: Bodleian 8° I 22. Jur. (4); Harvard Beale T220.

Notes: STC 20897; Beale T220; Dibdin 859; University Microfilms 142.

41   *True Copy of the Ordinance*

This is a true Copy of thordinaunce. c.1527-1528. 8°. Reprinted by Robert Redman and others; see Beale T232-T246 and STC 7695.5 - 7704.

Title: **¶This a true Copy of thordinaūce made in** | **the tyme of the reygne of kynge Henri the. vi. to** | **be obſeruyd in the kynges Exchequier by thoffy** | **cers and clerkes of the ſame for takynge of Fees** | **of the kynges accomptaūtȝ in the ſame Courte.** | [woodcut of Royal Arms, 46x50, as described in 37]

Collation: 8°, A^8, 8 unnumbered leaves; $4 signed [rotunda].

Contents: A1: title. A1^v: "**¶In thoffyce** ...", text to A8^v: "**Finis.**".

Type: text (A6) 28 11., 93 (96) x 67; 67 rotunda.

Examined: Bodleian 8° I 22. Jur. (5); Harvard Beale T232.

Notes: STC 7695.5; Beale T232; Dibdin 859; University Microfilms 1813.

42   *Curiam Baronis*

Modus tenendi Curiam Baronis. c.1527-1528. 8°. Reprinted from earlier editions by Pynson and others; see Beale T180-T201 and STC 7705.7 to 7721.

Title: **Modus tenend̄ Cur̄ Baron̄ cum | viſu franc' plegii.** | [woodcut of Royal Arms, 46x50, as described in 37]

Collation: 8°, A-B^8 16 unnumbered leaves; $4 signed, misprinting B1 (E1) [rotunda].

Contents: A1: title (verso blank). A2: "**Modus tenend̄ Cur̄ Baron̄ cum vi= | ſu Franc' plegii.** | **I**[lombardic cap^3]N ...", text to B8^v: "**F I N I S**".

Type: text (B1) 28 11., 93 (96) x 67; 67 rotunda.

Examined: Bodleian 8° I 22. Jur. (6), wanting C4; Harvard Beale T186.

Notes: STC 7712; Beale T186; Dibdin 859; University Microfilms 78. The revised STC notes that this book "Should collate A-B^8, w. B1^r line beginning: R.B. grit'; all copies have quires B-C belonging to 7727".

43   *Abridgment of Statutes*

John Rastell, *Abridgement of Statutes*. 22 December 1527. 8°. Reprinted from Rastell's edition of 1519 (11).

No title or implicit.

Colophon: **¶Enprynted in the chepeſyde at the ſyg= | ne of the mere mayde next to poulys ga= | te the .xxii. day of Deceber in the .xix | yere of the reyngne of oure ſo | uerayne lorde kinge Henry | the .viii. | ¶Per me Iohannem Raſtell | A.D. MDXXVII. | Cum Priuilegio Regali.**

Collation: 8°, πA^8 a-z^8 &^{8} A-I^8, 272 leaves foliated [1-8] **i-lv vi lvii-lxxxvi lxxvii lxxxviii-clxxxix xc clxxx-cclxi cclx [in one state] cclxii-cclxiiii (=272)**; $3 (-$\pi$A2-4, lo3) signed, misprinting I4 (E4) in one state [textura, πA lombardic capital].

RT: **Folliū .i. on al, followed by variations Fol., Fo., Fo?.** to end, in no significant pattern.

Contents: πA1: **"The ſtatutes | Prohemium Iohannis Raſtell. | B[lom-**bardic cap^2**]Ecauſe ...",** prologue to πA3. πA3^V: **"Tabula | Abiuracyon ...",** text in two columns to πA7: **"Finis Tabule".** πA7-A8^V: blank. al: **"Abiuracion Folliū .i. | H[lombardic cap^2]E ...",** text to I8: **"F I N I S."** | colophon. I8^V: [device McKerrow 37].

Type: Text (c2) 27 11., 90 (97) x 67; 67 rotunda, headings 93a textura.

Examined: British Library C.65.aa.13; Bodleian Tanner 102; Cambridge Syn. 8.52.19; Syn. 8.52.20 (Royal Library).

Notes: STC 9518; Beale S44; Cowley 11; Dibdin 834; University Micro-films 6. This book is roughly the same size as the volumes of the preceding set of legal texts, 37-42, and perhaps was meant to be part of a set with them.

On πA8^V there is an unlinked trace of a cut or device, presumably used as a bearer for the blank page.

44   St. Germain, *Doctor and Student*

[Christopher Saint Germain], *Dialogus de fundamentis legum Angliae et de conscientia*. 1528. 8°. Reprinted in 1604 for Thomas Wright (STC 21560). An English translation printed by Robert Wyer followed c.1530 (STC 21561), and was revised shortly afterwards (STC 21562). In English and with additions and a second English dialogue the work was frequently reprinted; see STC 21567-21582.5 and Beale T462-T480. In 1583 it became the property of Richard Tottell (Arber II.419).

Title: **¶Dialogus de | fundamentis | legum An= | glie et de | conſcientia**.

Colophon: **¶Explicit dialogus de fun= | damentis legum anglie & de conſci | entia. Impreſſum Londini p̱ | Iohannem Raſtell. An | no Dni. M.v.C. | .xxviii. | ¶Cum priuilegio Regali.**

Collation: 8°, A-L^8 M^4 χ^2, 94 leaves foliated "**Folio primo**" [in some copies] **ii-xci** [93-94] (=94); $4 (-M4) signed [textura].

Contents: A1: title. A1^V: "**¶Prologus | ¶Prefens dialogus ...**", to A2^V. A3: "**¶Introductio. | Q**[lombardic cap^3, small]**Vida̅...**", to A3^V: "**De lege eterna capitu .i. | ¶Doctor. Sicut** ...", text in 34 chapters to M3: "**Tabula**" to M4: "**Finis Tabule.**" | colophon. M4^V: [device McKerrow 37]. χ1: "**¶Errata.**" in single column to χ2. χ2^V: blank.

Type: text (F1) 22 11., 102 (111) x 69; 93a textura, headings 116 textura, title 220 textura.

Examined: Bodleian Crynes 868 (1); Bodleian 8° F 1 Jur.; British Library 506.a.1; Cambridge Syn. 8.52.12: Cambridge Syn. 8.52.38 (proof sheets or trial pulls for C1^{r-v} and C8^{r-v}, printed on only one side); O*.14.23 wanting M4 and the errata leaves χ1-2; Pet. E.2.50.; Harvard Beale T461 without the errata leaves; T462 with the errata leaves and with "Folio primo" on title.

Notes: STC 21559; Beale T461; T462; Dibdin 832; Sayle 347; University Microfilms 76. No copies are listed in the post-mortem inventory.

The 1523 edition noted in the successive editions of *Typographical Antiquities* (see Dibdin 831) seems to me to be a ghost, though one that keeps reappearing in legal history. The colophon design, with the ".xxviii." in its own line, could easily allow a misreading to occur, or there could have been a press variant state. More significantly, the 1528 edition was followed in only two years by an English translation and a second dialogue in English, and in three years by a compilation of additions, all suggesting that the book was very successful and that there was a demand for more of its discussion of matters of law and conscience.

There seems no reason why a book would have little effect in 1523 and so much five years later. No copies of a 1523 edition survive, while there are many copies of the 1528 edition, and indeed relatively large numbers of surviving copies of all the editions of this book.

A second dialogue in English was printed by Peter Treveris and published on 24 November 1530. Since Treveris did much of Rastell's printing for him in the late 1520's, it is tempting to assume that this edition was shared between the two men. But there is no evidence to support such an assumption, and all the many copies still extant bear the name of the Southwark printer.

The change to English was "for the profyte of the multytude" and the treatise was made for those "that be nat lerned in the law of this realme."

These two dialogues, which later acquired the abbreviated title *Doctor and Student,* had some importance in the intensifying Reformation crisis. An anti-clerical, perhaps mildly Erastian, tone is evident in the work, especially in the second dialogue. It was also important in the development and history of common law, as virtually all legal historians have noted.

The Latin dialogue, the English translation, and the English second dialogue were all published anonymously, but have been assumed from very early on to be the work of the lawyer and Reformation polemicist Christopher Saint Germain. All of the works attributed to Saint Germain were anonymous. Some of them, but not *Doctor and Student,* were listed in the last pages of Bale's Ipswich and Wesel edition of *Illustrium majoris Britanniae scriptorium summarium* (STC 1295 and another issue STC 1296) in 1548, but it is included in the expanded life in the 1559 Basel edition, at pp. 660-661. This revision is prefixed toThomas Wright's edition of 1604 (STC 21560), and the consensus among students since then seems to have been that it was indeed the first of several publications by a relatively aged lawyer, whose studies of the relationships between church law and the laws of England made him a valuable spokesman for the English Reformation.

Doctor and Student was kept in print as a textbook for a very long time. There was a modern edition by William Muchall (Cincinnati, 1874), and more recently the Selden Society edition edited by T.F.T. Plucknett and J.L. Barton (London, 1974). Valuable recent work on Saint Germain has also been done by J.A. Guy in another Selden Society book, *Christopher St German on Chancery and Statute* (London, 1985) and in his introduction to *The Complete Works of St. Thomas More,* 10, *The Debellation of Salem and Bizance* (New Haven and London, 1987). The historic and legal implications of the book are explored with great learning and clarity in these three studies. Also still of importance are Pearl Hogrefe's "The Life of Christopher Saint German," *Review of English Studies* 13 (1937), pp. 398-404, which demonstrates that Rastell and Saint Germain had been associated since 1502, Franklin L. Baumer's "Christopher St. German: the Political Philosophy of a Tudor Lawyer", *American Historical Review* 42 (1937), pp. 631-635, and S.E. Thorne's "St. Germain's *Doctor and Student,*" *The Library*, 4th ser. 10 (1929-30), pp. 421-6.

As can be seen from the bibliographical description above, the Rastell edition presents a few slight complications. Some copies have "Folio primo" on the title page, while others do not. C1.8, as represented by the proof sheet in the Cambridge University Library, exists in two different states. Some copies have the errata gathering χ^2, while some do not. There is no reason to expect any consistency in the appearance of one or more of these things in any one copy. Yet Plucknett and Barton apparently consider Beale T461, without the foliated title page, as not only a separate edition but one unique in the Harvard Law Library, and Guy states both categorically and incorrectly that "STC 21559 conflates two separate editions of this work by Rastell" (Guy, *Christopher St German*, p. 16).

45   *Abbreviation of Statutes*

John Rastell, editor, *Magnum abbreuiamentum statutorum Anglie vsque ad annum .xv. H. viii. inclusiue.* English, Law French, and Latin. Peter Treveris for Rastell. 1 December 1528. 8°.

Title: ¶**Magnum ab=** | **breuiamentū** | **ſtatutorum** | **Anglie** | **vſqꝫ ad an** | **num .xv. H. viii** | **incluſiue.**

Colophon: ¶**Iohānes Raſtel imprimi** | **me fecit .i. die Decembris** | **"anno dni. M.ccccc.** | **xxviii.** | **¶Cum priuilegio regali**

Collation: 8°, π^8 A-X^8 y-z^8 &^{8} a-g^8, 336 leaves foliated [1-8] **i-ccc.xxiii** [324-328] (=336); $4 signed [rotunda].

RT: follows text with "**Fo.**" and number; "**Fol.**" on AB1, B2, C3, A4, AB5-8.

Contents: π1: title (verso blank). π2: "¶**the prologe** | I[lombardic cap^2]N **this** ...", to π3. π3^v: "**Tabula**" in two columns to π8^v. A1: "**N**[lombardic cap^2]**Vlne**...", text to g6: colophon. g6^v: errata in single column to g8: "**Finis**". g8^v: [device McKerrow 37].

Type: text (P1) 30 11., 101 (107) x 68 (75 to numbers in outer margins); 67 rotunda, headings 93b textura, title 220 textura.

Examined: Cambridge SSS.47.12; Syn 8.52.14; Syn. 8.52.18; Harvard Beale S45.

Notes: STC 9620; Beale S45; Cowley 15; University Microfilms 133. The use of 93b textura implies that the printing was largely or completely done by Peter Treveris. The colophon includes the only dated use of the "fieri facias" formula, as used in 21,22, and 23. While the work is based on a number of earlier Abridgments of statutes, including Rastell's own (11 and 43), it differs in having the Abridgments made in the language of the original statute.

Though the work is anonymous, it contains all the marks of Rastell, particularly in the tone of the preface and the use of his beloved numbers of algorism. For the sake of simpler and wider reference, the preface says,

> two thynges be ordeyned and deuysyd, The fyrste is a table after the order of the lettres of the crossrew whych keapith an order to the second, thyrde, and fourthe lettre of the worde yf ther be so many lettres in it, and the same order also holdyth throughe all the boke of the pryncypal chapyters so that in maner the principal chapitres wyl be as soon founde in the boke as in the kelendre The seconde thynge is this, Vpon euery statute that ys abrygyd in any of the chapytres of thys book be set fygures of algorysme, *that* is to saye vppon the fyrste statute of the chapytre is set a fygure of one and vpon the seconde statute is set a fygure of two and so forth.

No copies are listed in the post-mortem inventory.

46   More, *Dialogue Concerning Heresies*

Sir Thomas More, *A dyaloge of syr Thomas More ... wherin be treatyed dyuers maters*. Completed by Peter Treveris after having been begun by Rastell. June 1529. Reprinted by William Rastell in 1531 (STC 18085) and edited by him in More's *English Works* in 1557 (STC 18076).

Title: ¶A dyaloge of ſyr Thomas | More knyghte : one of the | coun-ſayll of oure ſouerayne lorde the kyng | & chauncellour of hys duchy of Lan= | caſter. wherin be treatyd dyuers | maters/ as of the vener-ation | & worſhyp of ymagys & | relyques/ prayng to | ſayntys/ & goyng | o͞ pylgrymage. | wyth many othere | thyngys touchyng the | peſtylent ſect of Luther and | Tyndale/ by the tone bygone in | Sax-ony/ and by the tother | laboryd to be brought in | to Englond.˙.

Colophon: ¶Enpryntyd at London at the | ſygne of the meremayd at Pow= | lys gate next to chepe ſyde in the | moneth of Iune the yere of our | lord. M.v.C.xxix. | ¶Cum priuilegio Regali.

Collation: 2°, A^4 B-V,^{6} X-Y^4 χ^1, 127 leaves foliated [1] ii-lxxiii liiii lxxv-lxxxiiii lxxxvi lxxxvi lxxxviii lxxxii lxxxix xc-xcvii xxviii xcix-Cxxvi [127] (=127); $3 (-XY3) signed, misprinting K3 as H3 [tex-tura].

RT: Fo. with number to II^v: then The ſeconde [thyrde] [fourth] boke. Fo. . ſecondeboke. I3^v, 4^v; thvrd Nl, PQRI1^v, O2, NOQR2^v, NO3, OQR3^v, O4, P4^v, O5, OP5^v, O6^v.

Contents: A1: title. A1^v "The preface | ¶Hyt ys ...", to A2^{va}: "The furſt chapyter | ¶The ...", text in 31 chapters, each with heading, summary, and cap^2 or ^{3} to I1^{vb}: "¶The end of the | fyrſt boke.". I2^{ra}: "¶The ſec-onde | boke." | summary | "A[initial^7 33x33]Fter ...", text in 12 chapters as above to M3^{ra}: "¶The ende of the ſeconde | boke". M3^{r-b}: blank. M3^{va}: "¶The thyrde | boke," | summary | "A[initial^7 33x33]Bout ....," text in 16 chapters as above to R4^{va}: "¶The ende of the thyrd boke.". R4^{vb}: blank. R5^{ra}: "¶The fourthe | boke," | summary | "W[initial^7 29x33]Hen we ...", text in 18 chapters as above to Y4^{vb}. On Y4^v: "¶Finis." | [within a frame of ornamental strips from Treveris's stock, device McKerrow 37] | colophon. χ 1: "¶The fawtys eſcaped in the pryntynge.", in two columns to χ1^{vb}: "¶Finis.".

CW: A-B ys that [is that] B-C conſy= [conſydere] C-D ebbyng E-F through F-G in a G-H that H-I yes [¶Yes] I-K whyſpered [whiſpered] K-L longe L-M and M-N not N-O he geteth [he getteth] O-P vycyouſe [vyvyouſe.] P-Q vertouſe [vertuouſe] Q-R for the R-S yf god S-T dedys T-V was V-X ſay X-Y couered

Type: text (E3) 44 11., 204 (212) x140, two columns each 204x66; A-H, O2.4, 3.5, 93a textura; I-N, O1.6, P-Y, 93b textura; O2-O5^V have 46 or 47 lines to each page; headings 116 textura, first two lines of title 220 textura; errata and paste-in on Q4^V 54 textura.

Examined: Bodleian Douce M 739 title-leaf mounted and without errata; British Library C.37.h.10 device only from the Bagford collection; Folger STC 18084; Guildhall Cock collection 1.1.

Notes: STC 18084; Dibdin 838; Gibson 53; University Microfilms 896; English Experience 752.

There is a modern edition by Thomas M.C. Lawler, Germain Marc'hadour, and Richard C. Marius, *The Complete Works of St. Thomas More, 6, A Dialogue Concerning Heresies* (New Haven and London: Yale University Press, 1981), in two parts, text and apparatus.

More appears to have made two significant intrusions into the text after printing had begun, a troublesome business that More had shown himself quite capable of in the printing of the *Responsio ad Lutherum* in 1523, when he arrived at the King's Printer's house after the book was finished with a revised text.

The first problem is that Book I is not so designated until the heading and ending of the 31st and last chapter, and that in the middle of that chapter there is a change of type face to 93b textura, indicating that Rastell had passed the text over to Peter Treveris for completion. The only explanation of this that I can think of is that Rastell thought he was completing the printing of the whole work, at a time when he was trying to complete his own chronicle history and print it, and that More unexpectedly produced three more books, each considerably shorter than the first, leading to the use of Rastell's usual sub-contractor and the beginning of running titles specifying books from there on.

The second problem occurs in signature O, in which More has clearly expanded his arguments about Tyndale's rendering in the New Testament of the words "priest," "church," and "charity" as "senior," "congregation," and "love." This expansion seems to have involved setting the revised text in Rastell's shop, as shown by the use of his 93a textura, with two or more extra lines to a page, producing a new section of O2 to O5^V to fit within Treveris's O1.6; this is clearly identifiable by the longer pages and the consistent use of the running title form "thyrd," which is normally a variant, as can be seen in the bibliographical description. There appear to be no copies with the original text at this point in the book, which implies that the expansion took place before the work was complete and ready for sale.

An alternative possibility that a manuscript page got lost between two shops seems much less likely on several grounds: More had seriously revised a printed text before; the argument at the point in signature O where the longer pages occur is of great importance; and the addition, clearly by the author, of another expansion, presumably after the book was printed and again on a very important matter, is present in signature Q. The matter was that of the guilt or innocence of Dr. Horsey in the death of Richard Hunne, which had become a focus for resentment against the Church. On Q4^V there is a paste-in in the left margin by which More has added about 150 words of text. There are 33 lines of text in Treveris's 54 textura; the place of the text is marked by a manuscript dagger mark after the word "innocencye" in the first column of the page. Since no mention is made of it in the three errata, it was probably added at a very late point.

I have treated these alterations before in "Thomas More's Textual Changes in the *Dialogue Concerning Heresies*," *The Library*, 5th series, 27 (1972), pp. 233-235, and in the wider context of More's attitude towards the printing process in "Thomas More and his Printers," in *A Festschrift for Edgar Ronald Seary* (St. John's: Memorial University, 1975), pp. 40-57. The Yale editors disagree with me, and rather vehemently, but I am not convinced by their arguments and feel that claims such as that Rastell did not use running titles in Book 1 because he "simply did not think of using them even though he had the type to do so" make up not so much an argument as a *tussis pro crepitu*.

The single leaf of errata, printed on both sides, is not included with all surviving copies.

47   *Pastime of People*

John Rastell, *The Pastyme of People* or *The Cronycles of Englande and of dyuers other realmes*. 1529-1530. 2°.

Title: [letterpress title, presumably the earlier] **¶The Cronycles of Englande and of | dyuers other realmes: ' breuely com= | pyled with the pyctures and | armes of all the kynges | of Englande ſyth | the conqueſt | ','**

[xylographic title] [row of eight woodcuts, one of the 23x13 series and seven of the 23x23 series] | title woodcut, **The paſtyme of people** [22x16] | T[lombardic capital²]**he Cronycles of dyuers realmys and moſt ſpecyally of the realme of | Englond breuely copylyd & empryntyd in chepeſyde at the ſygne of | the mearemayd next to pollys gate. | ¶Cum priulegio.** | [two vertical leaf ornaments, seven woodcuts of the 23x23 series, two type ornaments] Variant arrangements probably occurred; at least one, with different woodcuts, exists.

Collation: 2°, A-E⁶, 30 unnumbered leaves; $6 signed, misprinting E2 as C2; ²A-²F⁶ ²G², 38 unnumbered leaves; $3 signed [textura].

RT: In the second part only, the names of the kings as they are discussed appear in the headlines as running titles; no variation of spelling or typography occurs within these.

Contents: A1: title. A1ᵛ: [after letterpress title] "**Prologus.**| W[open lombardic cap³]**ho ſo wyll rede** ...", to A2; [or after xylographic title] "**¶Prologus.** | I[lombardic cap²]**t is well affyrmyd** ...", to A2: [the texts are identical except in the openings and minor variations in spelling and the like; "**Iohannis Raſtell**" appears in the headline on A2, though the preface is not otherwise signed]. A2ᵛ: text, divided to allow readers to understand a period at once: on each page the prominent names are in factotums for emphasis, the sections are delineated by rows of type ornaments, and each part is marked in the margins on both sides as P (papal history), E (imperial history), B (British history), F (French history), and T (all other history). There are various woodcut illustrations, Hodnett 2290 to 2311. On E6ᵛ: "**¶Thus endeth the cronicles of eglod & of dyuers | other realmes vnto the tyme of king | wilm callyd the coqueror | whych was duke of | Normandy.**" | [three rows of type ornaments]. ²A1: "**¶wyllyam Conquerour.**" | [woodcut Hodnett 2312]. ²A1ᵛ: text divided as before, but without the factotums; each reign begins with a woodcut of the monarch (Hodnett 2312 for William I to 2329 for Edward V). There are 6 apparently borrowed initials, which were used by William Rastell in his 1533 edition of Robert Fabyan's *Chronicle*

(STC 10660). These are E 34x33. used on ^{2}C1, 3^v, 5^v, ^{2}F3, 6, and ^{2}G1^v; H 34x35, used on ^{2}A4, ^{2}B1, 5, ^{2}D6^v, ^{2}E2, 4; I 32x33, used on ^{2}B3; R 34x34, used on ^{2}B2, ^{2}D4; S 33x35, used on ^{2}A5; and W 33x32, used on ^{2}A1^v, 3. The similarity in size results only from their being planned for dropping six or seven lines into a pica or English text; they do not comprise a set. ^{2}G1^v: text ends without a finis. ^{2}G2: blank. ^{2}G2^v: [device McKerrow 37]. | **Cum privilegio Regali**.

Type: text (^{2}D2) 51 11. and five lines of type ornament, 269(277)x(167 in first part, 171 in second), 93a textura, headings and explicit of first part 116 textura, letterpress title and headings of large woodcuts 220 textura. Presumably because of the demand so large a book made on the type supply there is a greater than usual use of the alternate "ragged" r in the 93a textura, and the experimental th letter from *Book of the New Cards* (26) appears on A2.

Examined: Bodleian Douce add. c.2, imperfect; British Library C.15.c.6; G. 6030, with different arrangement of woodcuts on title; Cambridge Syn.3.52.1, very imperfect and wanting all second part; Huntington 82498, with letterpress title, wanting \$^{2}G, examined from photographic copy.

Notes: STC 20724; Dibdin 839; Sayle 353; University Microfilms 1713. There is an edition by T.F. Dibdin (London, 1811) and a modern edition by Albert J. Geritz (New York and London, 1985). Geritz's edition, *The Pastyme of People and A New Boke of Purgatory*, includes a facsimile of one of the British Library copies as well as a full transcript and an introduction, in which he discusses at length such matters as the typographical arrangement of the history, Rastell's skeptical treatment of some of his source material, and the overall dependence of the book on Robert Fabyan's *Chronicle*.

The date of the book is confirmed by a statement on ^{2}D6^v:

> After the deposynge of this kynge Rycharde, kyng Henry found great treasour, what in his treasourye & what in other places, in money & iewels, to the value of .vii.M.li. But yet here ye must note that .xl.s. in those dayes was better than .xl.s. is at this present day, which is nowe the .xxi. yere of kynge Henry the .viii. for at those dayes .v. grotes made an ounce, and nowe at this day .xi. grotes maketh an ounce.

The regnal year ended 21 April 1530, so it can be assumed that the work was begun and perhaps in part sold in late 1529 and completed in 1530.

The post-mortem inventory lists five copies of "the second part of the cronicles," worth 3|4, but no copies of the first part.

48   *New Book of Purgatory*

John Rastell, *A new boke of purgatory*, 10 October 1530. 2°. Reprinted by Rastell with same date (49).

Title: ⸿A new boke of purgatory | whiche is a dyaloge & dyſputacyon betwene | one [n inverted] ⸿Comyngo an Almayne a Chriſten man/ & one | ⸿Gyngemyn a turke of Machoinettſ law" dyſ= | putynge by nat- urall reaſon and good phi | loſophye/ whether there be a purga | torye or no purgatorye. which | boke is deuyded into thre | dyalogys. | .:. |⸿The fyrſt dyaloge ſheweth and treateth of the | merueylous exyſ- tens of god. | ⸿The ſeconde dyaloge treateth of the immorta= | lyte of mannys ſoule. | ⸿The thyrde dyaloge treateth of purgatory.

Colophon: ⸿Thus endeth thys lytell treatyſe͞ gedered and compyled by | Iohn͞ Raſtell. And alſo by the ſame Iohn͞ imprynted | and fully fynyſſhed/ the .x. day of October" ẙ yere | of our lord god. M. CCCCC. XXX. | ¶Cum priuilegio Regali.

Collation: 2°, a⁶ b-g⁴ h⁶, 36 unnumbered leaves; $3 (+a4) signed, mis- printing a2 as **A.ij.**, d3 as d4 [textura with arabic numerals].

RT: **The fyrſt dialoge.** | **of the merueylous exiſtens of god.; dialoge** b1ᵛ; **The ſeconde dialoge | of the immortalyte of mannes ſoule.; ⸿The thyrde dialoge | of purgatory.; The** gh1ᵛ, h3ᵛ, gh4ᵛ; **purgatorye** h1ᵛ; **Tabula.** h5-6.

Contents: a1: title. a1ᵛ: "⸿**The prologe of the author.** | **I**[initial⁷ 32x33]**T** ...", to a2ᵛ: "⸿**Finis prologi.**". | [chapter heading] | "**C**[initial⁸ 32x33]**Omyngo** ...", text under 17 headings, each beginning text cap², to b3ᵛ: "⸿**Thus endeth the fyrſt dyaloge" declarynge | the meruelous exyſtens of god.**॑.". b4: "⸿**The ſeconde dialoge of the immor | talyte of mannes ſoule.**" | [chapter heading] | "**G**[initial⁷ 32x32]**yngemyn.**", text under 22 headings as above to e3ᵛ: "⸿**Thus endeth the ſeconde dyaloge of the | immortalyte of mannes ſoule.**". e4: "⸿**The thyrde dialoge**" | [chapter heading]| "**C**[initial⁸ 32x33]**Omyngo.**" text under 15 headings as above to h4ᵛ: "॑.॑." | colophon. h5: "**Tabula.**", single column to h6: "⸿**Finis calendarij.**". h6ᵛ: [device McKerrow 37].

CW: a-b **¶That** b-c **tell me** c-d **yf the ſoule** [⸿**yf the ſoule**] d-e **hath no** e-f **god to** f-g **pure** g-h **god**

Type: text (h3) 43 11., 198 (210) x 128; 93a textura, headings 116 tex- tura, first line of title 220 textura.

Examined: Bodleian Mason Z 163; British Library C.111.g.10(3).

Notes: STC 20719; Dibdin 840; University Microfilms 140 and 141. See also the modern critical edition by Albert J. Geritz, *The Pastyme of People and A New Boke of Purgatory* (New York and London, 1985), with an excellent discussion of the book at pp. 32-51. I discussed the genesis and publication of the book as well in an article on "John Rastell's Press in the English Reformation," *Moreana* 49 (1976), pp. 29-47.

The completion date of 10 October indicates that the book followed directly after *Pastime of People,* and like it and More's *Dialogue of Heresies* results from a conviction of the now quite aged Rastell that his experience of the world, his knowledge of the law, and his membership in the Reformation Parliament, which began its work in the autumn of 1529, all compelled him to take an active part in the intellectual and moral development of the English people in a serious kind of way, different from the publication of cheerfully humanist works in small formats. The conviction was to have dire results.

Rastell's book on purgatory, following as it does the *Dialogue of Heresies*, implies a close relationship with his wife's brother More. Most obviously its structure is based on More's *Utopia,* a dialogue between a Christian but flawed Europe and a non-Christian but reasonable east from which much good could be learned, even if that good were based on reason rather than revelation. Therefore Rastell's semi-Lutheran German, named Comyngo for some reason, doubts the doctrine of purgatory, but it is firmly re-established by his implacably logical Moslem, Gyngemyn, who claims that the belief that souls go to Heaven or Hell without a Purgatory

> was but folysh and agayns all good naturall reason, bycause that all people in *the* world of what contrey so euer they haue be or be, of what law or secte so euer they haue be or be, aswel the Panyms, the Iewes, and you that be of Chrystes fayth, & we that be of Machomets law, and all other that euer lyued or do lyue after the order of any good reason, haue euer byleued and do byleue that there is a purgatory, where mannes soules shall be purged after this mortal lyfe.

So clear is this natural reason in Rastell's mind that the two agree to argue the matter without any texts from the Bible or the Koran or any of the commentators. The setting of the dialogue in a group of merchants meeting in a "great cytye" is also imitated from More, as are its basic assumptions about the existence of God, the immortality of the soul, and reward or punishment after death—the foundations of the Utopian pleasure principle.

Rastell seems remarkably ill-informed about the dispute on justification. Purgatory was not a doctrine held in all faiths, by any means, and Rastell's ideas about why the doctrine had been challenged are peculiar as well. The first reason, that repentance is sufficient in itself, was to the point. That the infinite nature of life after death precluded a temporal purgatory; that God would apportion felicity or suffering according to each soul's deserts; that the sin-stained saved could take lower places in Heaven; that suffering for sin should occur in this life; that repentance would be complete in itself; and that offenses done to neighbours would be totally forgiven by God without any compensation required were all different questions indeed. Though the Turk said he could soon answer them all "by natural reason & good phylosophye," they had not in fact been raised by any of the reformers.

Not using any texts could well have been the greatest error; no reformer would even consider a doctrinal argument without Scripture, and, as John Frith wrote of Rastell's book, a work treating justification without the words of Christ "lyethe all readye in the dirte."

The response of Frith to the books of Fisher, More, and Rastell evoked another response, now lost, from Rastell and visits to the young reformer after his arrest in 1532, which led finally to Rastell's own conversion.

That a second edition, unfortunately with the same date, was printed suggests that the book had some success. No copies are listed in the post-mortem inventory, which could mean they had all been sold or perhaps even given away by Rastell—which is unlikely for a fairly substantial folio—or that he got rid of them when he changed his belief.

49

[another edition] *A new boke of purgatory.* 10 October 1530. 2°. Reprinted from 48 above.

Title: ⁊A new boke of purgatory | whiche is a dyaloge & dyſputacyon betwene | one ⁊Comyngo an Almayne a Chriſten man/ & one | ⁊Gyngemyn a turke of Machionettſ law/ dyſ= | putynge by naturall reaſon and good phi | loſphye" whether there be a purga | torye or no purgatorye. which | boke is deuyded into thre | dyalogys. | .:. | ⁊The fyrſt dyaloge ſheweth and treateth of the | merueylous exyſtens of god. | ⁊The ſeconde dyaloge treateth of the immorta= | lyte of mannys ſoule. | ¶The thyrde dyaloge treateth of purgatorye.

Colophon: ⁊Thus endeth thys lytell treatyſe/ gydered and compyled by | Iohn̄ Raſtell. And alſo by the ſame Iohn̄ imprynted | and fully fynyſhed" the .x. daye of october/ $\stackrel{e}{y}$ yere | of our lord god M.CCCC. XXX. | ⁊Cum priuilegio Regali.

Collation: 2°, a⁶ b-g⁴ h⁶, 36 unnumbered leaves; $3 (+ah3) signed textura with roman numerals.

RT: ⁊The fyrſte dyaloge. | of the merueylous exiſteus of god.; exiſtens a5, 6, b1-3; The fyrſt dialoge. a6ᵛ; [small paragraph mark] The fyrſte dyaloge. b1ᵛ, 3ᵛ; Of the marueylous exiſtens of god.∴b2; ⁊The ſecond dyaloge. | of the immortalyte of mannis ſoule; ⁊The ſeconde dialoge cd1ᵛ, 2ᵛ; of the immortalyte of mannis ſoule c2; of the immortalyte of mannis ſoule. cde3, cd4; ⁊The ſecond dyaloge. d4ᵛ; ⁊The thyrd dyaloge. | of purgatorye.; dialoge fghlᵛ, 2ᵛ, h3ᵛ; Tabula. h5ʳ⁻ᵛ, 6.

Contents: al: title. alᵛ: "⁊The prologe of the auctor. | I[initial⁷ 32x33]T ...", to a2ᵛ: "⁊Finis prologi.:.", a3: "⁊The fyrſt dialoge of the marueylous | exiſtens of god.∴" | [chapter heading] | "C[initial⁷ 32x33]Omyngo ...". text under 17 headings, each beginning text or lombardic cap², to b3ᵛ: "⁊Thus endeth the fyrſte dialoge declarynge | the meruelous exiſtens of god.∴". b4: "⁊The ſeconde dialoge of the immor | talyte of mannis ſoule." | [chapter heading] | "G[initial⁷ 32x33]yngemyn.", text under 22 headings as above to e3ᵛ: "Thus endeth the ſeconde dialoge of the | immortalyte of mannys ſoule.∴". e4: "The thyrd dyaloge." | [chapter heading]. "C[initial⁷ 32x 33]Omyngo ...", text under 15 headings as above to h4ᵛ: colophon in H.J. Graham copy, but only the privilege in the Balliol and Folger copies. h5: "Tabula." | single column to h6. h6ᵛ [device McKerrow 37 in H.J. Graham copy, blank in Balliol and Folger copies].

CW: a-b ¶**That** b-c **tell me** e-d **yf the ſoule** [ꝺyf the ſoule] d-e **hath no** e-g **god to** f-g **pure** g-h **god**

Type: text (hl) 43 11., 198 (210) x 128; 93a textura, headings 116 textura, first line of title 220 textura.

Examined: Oxford, Balliol 535.d.13(5); Howard Jay Graham copy, examined for me by Mr. Graham.

Notes: STC 20719.5 and 20720; University Microfilms for 20720 is 1358.

Statutes 21 Henry VIII. c.1531. 2°. Reprinted by Rastell in the same year (51).

Title: S[woodcut letter[6], 110x150, of man-faced dragon forming the initial above xylographic "**tatuta**" and dropped into text] | **In parliamento | apud weſtmonaſ ↓ terium tertio | die Nouēbris. Anno regni me= | tuendiſſimi Anglie et Francie | regis/ fidei defenſoris | ac domi | ni Hibernie Henrici octaui viceſimo primo Tento/ Bonū publicū | concernientia.**

Collation: 2°, A-D[4] E[6],22 unnumbered leaves; $3 (+E4) signed [textura].

RT: **Anno .xxi. Henrici octaui.** [both rectos and versos]; **Anno xxi. Henrici octaui** CDE1, BDE2, D3, A3[v], ACD4, E5, 6; **Anno xxi. Henrici octaui.** B1, C2; [none] D3[v]; **Anno .xxi. Henrici octaui.** E3[v], 4[v], 5[v].

Contents: A1 title. A1[v]: "**Anno .xxi. Henrici Octaui. | ¶Tabula.**" | single column. A2: "**¶Anno .xxi. Henrici Octaui. | T**[initial[7] 33x33]**He ...**", texts of 21 acts, each beginning lombardic cap[2], on D2[v] a text-size drop cap[5], or initials, B[8] 32x33 on A3[v], I[7] 33x34 on C4[v], P[4] 18x19 on D1[v], H[8] 34x35 on D2[v], W[7] 31x32 on E3, 4. On E6: "**¶Cum priuilegio regali.**". E6[v]: [within a frame of ornamental strips, left 14, upper 4, right 8, lower 13, 152x125 enclosing 128x94 device McKerrow 37].

CW: A-B **or teſtamentes [or teſtamētes]** B-C **hyghnes** C-D **[con=] teynynge [teynyng]** D-E **by theyr [ſayd ſentwary]**

Type: text (A3) 46 11., 216 (226) x151, 93a textura, headings 93a textura, RT 116 textura, first line of HT and Tabula 220 textura.

Examined: British Library 505.g.13, with title mounted.

Notes: STC 9363.6, formerly 9366; Beale S129 does not distinguish between this edition and 51; University Microfilms 56.

51

[another edition] *Statutes 21 Henry VIII.* c.1531. 2°. Reprinted from 50 above, or possibly so; there is no firm evidence by which the priority of either edition can be demonstrated.

Title: S[woodcut letter[6], 110x150, of man-faced dragon forming the initial above xylographic "**tatuta**" and dropped into text] | **In parliamento | apud weſtmonaſterium tertio | die Nouēbris. Anno regni me= | tuendiſſimi Anglie et Francie | regis/ fidei defenſoris" ac domi | ni Hibernie Henrici octaui viceſimo primo Tento/ Bonū publicum | con-cernientia.**

Collation: 2°, A-D[4] E[6], 22 unnumbered leaves; \$3 (+E4) signed [textura].

RT: **Anno .xxi. Henrici octaui.** [both rectos and versos].

Contents: A1: title. A1[v]: "**Anno .xi. Henrici octaui. | ¶Tabula,**" | single column. A2: "**¶Anno, xxj. Henrici octaui, |** T[initial[7] 33x33]**He ...**", texts of 21 acts, each beginning lombardic cap[2] or text-size drop cap[3] or initials. B[7] 23x33 on A3[v], I[7] 33x34 on C4[4], P[4] k5x15 on D1[v], H[8] 34x35 on D2[v], H[7] 28x28 on E2, W[6] and [7] 28x34 on E3, 4. On E6: "**Cum pri-uilegio regali.**". E6[v]: [device McKerrow 37].

CW: A-B **or teſtamentes [or teſtamet℥ B-C highnes C-D [con=] tey-nynge [teynyng] D-E ſentwary**

Type: text (D3) 46 11., 216 (226) x151, 93a textura, headings 93a textura, RT 116 textura, first line of HT and Tabula 220 textura.

Examined: British Library C.54.f.6; C.112.f.8, in which it forms the 21 Henry VIII section of *The great boke of statutes* (STC 9286).

Notes: STC 9363.8; Beale S129; University Microfilms 1792. An important bibliographic study is Howard Jay Graham's "'Our Tong Maternall Maruellously Amendyd and Augmentyd': the first Englishing and Printing of the Medieval Statutes at Large, 1530-1533," *UCLA Law Review* 13 (1958), pp. 58-98.

There are twelve copies in the post-mortem inventory, valued at a penny each (Roberts 1).

52   *Great Abridgment of Statutes*

John Rastell, *The grete abregement of the statutys of Englond vntyll the ,xxij, yere of kyne Henry the ,viij,*. 1531-1532. Printed by William Rastell for himself and John Rastell; edited and expanded by John Rastell from 11 and 43.

Title: ¶**The grete ab= | bregement of the | statutys of En= | glond vntyll | the ,xxij, yere | of kyng | Henry the ,viij, | Cum priuilegio | Regali, ' ,**

Collation: 8°, ^{8} a-B^8 a-z^8 &^{8} ^{2}A-^{2}O^8, 328 leaves foliated [1-24] **i-xxxiii xxxiiiii xxxv-ccxxxix cclx ccxli-ccxciii** [294-304] (=328); $5 (- Bfmt^{2}N4, Bp5) signed, misprinting c5 as .v. [bastard, A-B^8 with arabic numerals].

RT: In A-B^8 **Anno .xxii. | Henrici octaui; Henrici** A4; verso form on B1; **Anno .xxij. Henrici octaui:** B8^V; from a1 follows the text by subject.

Contents: 1: title.   1^V: ¶**Prohemium Iohannis Raſtell.**" | text as in 1519, beginning **B**[initial^7 23x22]**Ecauſe ...**", to   3, on which addition begins "**A**[lombardic cap^2]**Lſo ...**", to   3^V.   4: "**Tabula.**", in two columns to   8^V: "*FINIS TABVLAE.*". A1: "**The abregemēt | of the ſtatutys made in the | parlyamēt holden in | the .xxij. yere of | the | rayne of | kynge Henry | the | eyght. | .·.**". A1^V "**The table.**", single column. a2: "**T**[initial^6 18x21]**He ...**", text for 22 Henry VIII to B8^V: **Cum priuilegio.**". a1: "**N**^{10}[initial 32x36]**One ...**", text under legal headings in alphabetical order, each section beginning lombardic or less frequently textura cap inset 2, 3, or 4 lines, to ^{2}N6: alphabetical list of expired statutes to ^{2}N7^V. ^{2}N8: alphabetical list of authorities given in the realm to ^{2}O5^V: "*FIN*^{s}IS". ^{2}O6: statutes newly abridged to ^{2}O8: "*FIN*^{s}IS. | *CV*^{s}M PRIV^{s}ILEGIO | REGALI.*". ^{2}O8^V: blank.

CW: A-B **landys** a-b **ys not** b-c **his contrey [his contreye]** c-d ꝗ **A** d-e ſhy [ryffes] e-f the f-g **R.ii. [Richardi .ii.]** g-h **yf he** h-i ꝗ **Cuſtomers** i-k ꝗ **Clothys** k-l **Enymyes [Enemies in RT]** l-m **ſhall be [ſhalbe]** m-n **extorcyon** n-o **Fynours** [in RT on ol] o-p **And** p-q **Hoſpyta**l [**Hoſpytall** in RT] q-r ꝗ**Iuſtyces [**ꝗ**Iuſtyces]** r-s **in** s-t **made** t-v **to what** v-x **vt ſupra** [**vt ſupra.**] x-y **hym** y-z **[ex]cuſe them** z-& **ware [made]** &-^{2}A ¶**The** ^{2}A-^{2}B **Edward [E.iii.]** ^{2}B-^{2}C **[tre]ble dama [ble damages]** ^{2}C—^{2}D **hens** ^{2}D-^{2}E **Ryuers** [in RT on ^{2}E1] ^{2}E-^{2}F **v. yere** ^{2}F-^{2}G **[be] fore** ^{2}G-^{2}I **vnkno= [wynge]** ^{2}I-^{2}K ꝗ**Englyſ [**ꝗ**Englyſhmen]** ^{2}K-^{2}L **[far=] thyng** ^{2}L-^{2}M **Edward [Edwarde]** ^{2}M-^{2}N **refuſe** ^{2}N-^{2}O **To the**

Type: text (^{2}B1) 32 11., 107 (116) x 70 (73 to numerals in outer margins), 68 bastard, headings 102 bastard (William Rastell's types).

Notes: STC 9521; Beale S48, S82; Cowley 19, 21; University Microfilms 6. The type and design indicate clearly enough that the book was printed by William Rastell, but the expansion of the preface from the 1519 version and the continuing Abridgment of recent statutes suggest that he was printing for or in partnership with his father. The year 22 Henry VIII ended on April 1531, and presumably the Abridgment was done within the next twelvemonth. The 1538 inventory lists eight copies of "bregementes of statutes in English" worth 2/8, which could be this or 43 above (Roberts 2).

Though the new STC raises the possibility that William might have edited this book as well as having printed it, the expanded preface has a very distinct air of John Rastell, especially in the "fygures of algorysme" used to number the abridged statutes. Five innovations occur in the editing: there is an alphabetical index, the abridged statutes in each chapter are numbered with "fygures of algorysme" to help in cross-reference, there is a titled list of expired statutes, there is a list of authorities delegated to various persons in the realm, and finally there is a list of newly abridged statutes.

53

John Rastell, "A Second Book of Purgatory." Written and probably printed in 1532; lost, and perhaps destroyed by Rastell after his conversion, but refuted by John Frith in *An other boke against Rastel* (STC 11385). An incomplete statement under a heading from this book occurs on the verso of a deposition in one of Rastell's lawsuits, PRO Req. 2/8/14.

54

Map of Europe. c.1532.

Nothing is known of this woodcut map of Europe except that 110 copies were listed in the inventory of 1538 (Roberts 3), at 9/2, or a penny each. Rastell's cosmographical interests dated back many years.

55   Thibault, *Prognostication*

John Thybault, *Pronostycacyon*. Peter Treveris for Rastell. 1533. 4°. Translator unknown.

Title: ¶**Pronoſtycacyon of mayſter | Iohn̄ Thybault | medycyner and aſtronomer of the Emperyall | maieſtie/ of the yere of our lorde god .M.CCCC.xxxiii. co͞prehen= | dynge the .iiii. partes of this yere | and of the influence of the | mone/ of peas and warre | and of the ſyke- neſſes of this | yere" ẘ the conſtellacions of them ʒ̆ be vnder | the .vii. planettes | and the reuolucions of | kynges and princes | and of the | Eclyppes and Comete. | ⁌•✲•⁌ | [woodcut Hodnett *2286ᵇ]**

Colophon: ¶**Imprinted by me Iohn̄ Raſtell. | Cum priuilegio regali.**

Collation: 4°, $A1^4$, 4 unnumbered leaves; unsigned.

Contents: $A1$: title. $A1^v$: "¶**To the reder.** | I[initial[7] 32x35]T ...", text to $A4^v$: "¶**Finis.**" | colophon.

·Type: text ($A4$) 36 11., 168 x122; 93b textura, first line of title 220 textura.

Examined: British Library Bagford fragments, Harleian 5937 27/35/44/266; and 8610.b.53: both fragmentary, the former having the colophon pasted in at the bottom of the title page.

Notes: STC 517.12, formerly 23952; Bosanquet XVIII; University Microfilms 154. This seems to be simply a trade book; if there is something in the text that Rastell thought significant for his disputes or the workings of the Reformation Parliament, I have been unable to find it.

The 93b type identifies Treveris.

56

John Rastell, "The Church of Rastell." c.1533-1535.

Notes: That this lost work was both printed and of a reforming tendency is shown by the only evidence of its existence, Bishop Stephen Gardiner's prohibition of the book. See Gilbert Burnet, *The History of the Reformation of the Church of England,* 4 (Oxford, 1865), pt. i, bk. iii, no. xxvi.

57

John Rastell, "The Book of Charge." 1534, if printed, which seems unlikely.

Notes: This book was intended by Rastell to establish uniformity of religion in England, as indeed a later series of books by others in the reign of King Edward did. It seems never to have been actually printed, but to have been circulated at court, and sent back to Rastell for changes. Rastell hoped that the King would pay him to print "x or xij m" copies to be distributed free, and felt that this could be done "vnder the cost of C li.".

The book was discussed by Rastell in his last letters to Cromwell: PRO SP1/85/2885 and PRO SP1/85/4796.

58   *Primer*

John Rastell, *Primer.* 1534-1535, if printed.

Notes: Rastell's final attempt to reform the church and the world was the composition of "certeyn prayers to be put in primers of dyuers sortes of small price"; again he hoped that that the King would pay him to print four or five thousand to be distributed among the people, which would "not cost aboue C li," and would lead the people to correct doctrine.

The proposal was made in a letter to Cromwell, PRO SP1/85/2885.

At the inventory post-mortem of Rastell's house 787 copies of a *Primer* in English were listed (Roberts 7, and his note on the *Primer* at p. 42).

59

John Rastell, "Concordance with Table." In process at his death, and probably never completed.

Notes: In his will, made 20 April 1536, Rastell twice asserted the importance he attached to this book. First he bequeathed to his servant Thomas Wilson "besides his wages lyuery and borde" the sum of one pound "after my deceas assoon as my concordaunce and the table thereof is fynished and fayre written to hym to be printed." Second he requested his executor Ralph Cressey to support Wilson until "the said concordaunce bee fayre written and the table to print, and also to print the said concordaunce and table." Since Cressey would not act as executor and the estate would obviously not bear such an expense, the concordance seems to have disappeared.

What it was is another question. Certainly it would not have been the well-known alphabetical arrangement of the words of a book, which would not have required a table, but would have been what the note in the second edition of *OED* calls "a *real* concordance which is an index of *subjects* or *topics*". Alternately Rastell could have had the meaning *sb.* 5 in mind, "A composition combining and harmonizing various accounts." *OED* cites for this meaning Fabyan, a book Rastell most certainly knew. The subject is not specified either; it could have been a further revision of the Statutes, or a collection of legal or scriptural citations to favour the reformation. All that is really known is that Rastell completed it in rough copy.

Uncertain Books

Besides the books that Rastell published or wrote or edited, there are some books that he might have done or hoped to do about which some information exists. These are in three groups: books on the Catholic side of the reformation dispute, listed by John Pits, who of course ignored Rastell's conversion; books on the reformed side, listed by John Bale, who of course emphasized it; and a list of booklets Rastell proposed to Cromwell as a means of swaying minds before bringing a series of reformation bills into Parliament.

John Pits's *Relationum Historicarum de Rebus Anglicis Tomus Primus* (Paris, 1619) has an account of Rastell at pp. 725-726, which lists along with extant books five titles of works that seem to have an anti-reformation purpose. While these accord with Pits's intention of countering the influence of Bale on English bibliography, none of the books seems to exist, and the use of Latin short titles creates some confusion. The books could well have been written during the debate on Purgatory, and possibly destroyed by Rastell after his conversion led him to devote his press completely, as he told Cromwell, to books against the Pope.

60

De societate Rosarij. There is nothing in Rastell's whole body of writings to suggest a devotion to this specific form of prayer.

61

Regulas bonae vitae Anglice. It is quite possible that Rastell wrote such a book, perhaps during the period between 1525 and 1530.

62

De indulgentijs. The matter of indulgences seems not very large in Rastell's arguments for Purgatory, since they were based on natural reason, but it is at least possible that he wrote such a book in his controversy with John Frith.

63

De oratione. There is no other evidence that Rastell wrote any book on prayers except his reformed Primer.

64

De bonis operibus. Such a book could have been written as part of the debate on Purgatory, in which Rastell did bring up the problem of salvation by works.

John Bale's *Illustrium majoris Britanniae scriptorum summarium* (STC 1295) has its extensive list of Rastell's books at 3k2, including three books I have been unable to find, two of them seemingly reformation tracts.

65

Abundans gratia potentiae diuinae. This could be one of the "dyuers bok*es*" against the papacy and the old church that Rastell told Cromwell he had devoted his time and business to since his conversion.

66

Abrasionem papismi. Like 64, this would be an attack on the papacy, written and printed by Rastell.

67

Astrologicus canonicis. It is uncertain what this could be, a treatise by Rastell or simply a reference to (55) above.

Finally, Rastell in a memorandum to Cromwell about his hopes for the circulation of "the book of the charge" (*L&P* 7, 1043; PRO SP1/85, p. 47) proposed a series of books to be printed and circulated. Clearly he hoped to have the printing of these books. As so often in his life he anticipated what others would do successfully, in his idea for something like the later two books of *Homilies*:

> Item for the contyuaunce of true doctrine there wold be dyuers grete clerkes appoyntyd & hyryd by the kynges grace to take the payn to draw sermones in englyssh vppon euery gospell in the yere & those to be printyd & send vnto euerry curate commaundyng them to prech these same sermons eueury sonday or elles to reede them or the boke in the pulpit these thynges intendid shortly to be made & printyd ffyrst a lityll boke not past one shete of papyr to be compilyd & printyd before the parliament begynne, argueing & prouyng that prestes by the law of god may haue lyberte to take wyff of theyr own, & to haue liberte to work for theyr lyffyng Item that a nother lyke lytel boke be compylyd & printyd argueing & prouyng that by goddes law that men ought to honour no ymages or offer vnto them Item that a nother lyke lytyl boke be compilyd & printyd argueing & prouyng that the prayers of men that be here lyfyng for the soulis of them that be deed can in no wyse be profitable to them that be dede nor can not help them

The books on clerical celibacy and employment and on images were to be followed by bills in Parliament.

Possible Additions

STC Number	Date	Description
9895	1509	Yearbook - 1 Ed. V & 1 Ric. III
18361	1512	Narrationes
4077c.55A	1518	Indulgence - Hospital of St. Katherine's by the Tower
14077c.50	1519	Indulgence - General
22153	1525	Seeing of Urines - Rastell for Bankes
22153a	1526	Seeing of Urines - Rastell for Bankes
24199	1526	Treasure of Poor Men - Rastell for Bankes
7542.5	1528	Eglamour - speculated Rastell for Bankes
7773	1529	Proclamations - 21 Henry VIII - Treveris for Rastell
9533.2	1530	Abridgment of Statutes - 21 Henry VIII
17324.5	1530	Life of St. Margaret of Scotland
22607	1530	Skelton. Magnyfycence. Treveris for Rastell
23663(A3)	1530	A C Mery Tales
6800.3	1532	A Dyalogue Betwene One Clemente a Clerke
5892	1535	Goostly Psalms—J. Gough in the shop of J. Rastell

Note on STC 9895 (UM 64), STC 18361 (UM 483) and STC 22607 (UM 483): The first two of these, 9895 and 18361, are not claimed by Rastell nor does his name appear in them. I take it they are thought perhaps to be Rastell because the types resemble ones Rastell is known to have had in use at the time. A lot more evidence might be assembled to attribute 9895, because it contains several woodcuts; 18361 appears to be completely free from ornamentation. The third item, STC 22607, is a mistake on the part of University Microfilms and the Cambridge University Library; the item on the film is simply not a copy of the unique edition of Skelton's *Magnifycence*. It is a prose history beginning at the time of Brut. The Library may have been misled because at the top of the first leaf of the item photographed occurs the name of John Rastell; however, he is described in the third person as having come into possession of the work being printed. The presswork looks to me to be totally unlike Rastell. (Alan Somerset)

SELECTION OF MODERN RASTELL STUDIES

Primary Sources - Editions

Calisto and Melebea

The Interlude of Calisto and Melebea, ed. W.W. Greg and Frank Sidgwick. Oxford: Malone Society Reprints, 1908. Facsimile.

An Interlude of Calisto and Melebea (for the First Time Accurately Reproduced from the Original Copy) Printed by John Rastell, c. 1530, ed. Herbert Warner Allen. London: G. Routledge, 1908.

The Four Elements

The Interlude of the Four Elements, ed. James O. Halliwell. London: Richards, 1848. [Early English Poetry, Ballads, and Popular Literature of the Middle Ages, vol. 22].

Das 'Interlude of the Four Elements,' mit einer Einleitung, ed. Julius Fischer. Marburg: N.G. Elwert, 1903.

Interlude of the Four Elements, in *Siberch Celebrations, 1521-1971*, ed. Brooke Crutchley. Cambridge: University Printing House, 1971, pp. 81-113.

A New Interlude...Of the Four Elements, ed. John S. Farmer, Tudor Facsimile Text. London and Edinburgh, 1908, repr. New York, 1970.

John Rastell: The Four Elements as Performed at the University Printing House, Cambridge, ed. Roger Coleman. Cambridge: University Press, 1971.

The Four Elements and *Calisto and Melebea*

A Selection of Old English Plays [originally published by Robert Dodsley in 1744], vol. 1, pp. 1-92, ed. W. Carew Hazlitt. London: Reeves and Turner, 1874. Repr. New York, Benjamin Bloom, 1964.

*Six Anonymous Plays, First Series (1510 - 1537), Early English Dramatist*s, pp. 1-87, ed. John S. Farmer. London: Early English Drama Society, 1905. Repr. Guildford, England, 1966.

Gentleness and Nobility

Authorship and Sources of 'Gentleness and Nobility': A Study in Early Tudor Drama Together with a Text of the Play, ed. Kenneth W. Cameron. Raleigh, North Carolina: The Thistle Press, 1941.

Gentleness and Nobility, ed. John S. Farmer, Tudor Facsimile Text. Amersham, England, 1914.

Gentleness and Nobility, ed. A.C. Partridge and F.P. Wilson. Oxford: University Press, 1949. Facsimile.

The Spider and the Fly Together with an Attributed Interlude Entitled Gentleness and Nobility by John Heywood, ed. John S. Farmer. London: Early English Drama Society, 1908.

Pastime of People

A Critical Edition of John Rastell's 'The Pastyme of People' and 'A New Boke of Purgatory,' ed. Albert J. Geritz. New York: Garland Publishing, 1985. [The Renaissance Imagination, vol. 14].

The Pastime of People, ed. Thomas F. Dibdin. London: F.C. and J. Rivington, 1811.

The Four Elements, Calisto and Melebea, Gentleness and Nobility

Three Rastell Plays, ed. Richard Axton. Cambridge: D.S. Brewer, 1979. Old-spelling text.

Secondary Sources

Baskervill, C.R. "John Rastell's Dramatic Activities." *Modern Philology* 13 (1916): 557-60.

Bernard, Jules E., Jr. *The Prosody of the Tudor Interlude*. New Haven: Yale University Press, 1939. Repr. Archon Books, 1969.

Bevington, David. *Tudor Drama and Politics: A Critical Approach to Topical Meaning.* Cambridge: Harvard University Press, 1968.

Borish, M.E. "Source and Intention of *The Four Elements*." *Studies in Philology* 35 (1938): 149-63.

Brennan, Gillian. "Patriotism, Language and Power: English Translations of the Bible, 1520-1580." *History Workshop* 27 (1989): 18-36.

Brooke, C. Tucker. "*Gentleness and Nobility*: The Authorship and Source." *Modern Language Review* 6 (1911): 458-61.

Cartwright, Kent. "The Humanism of Acting: John Heywood's *The Foure PP.*" *Studies in the Literary Imagination* 26 (1993): 21-46.

Davies, Hugh W. *Devices of the Early Printers, 1475 - 1560: Their History and Development with a Chapter on Portrait Figures of Printers.* London: Grafton and Co., 1935.

Devereux, E.J. "John Rastell's Press in the English Reformation." *Moreana* 49 (1976): 29-47.

———. "John Rastell's Text of *The Parliament of Fowls.*" *Moreana* 27/28 (1970): 115-20.

———. "John Rastell's Utopian Voyage." *Moreana* 51 (1976): 119-23.

———. "Thomas More and his Printers." In *A Festschrift for Edgar Ronald Seary*, ed. A.A. Macdonald, P.H. O'Flaherty, and G.M. Story, St. John's: Memorial University, 1975, pp. 40-57.

———. "Thomas More's Textual Changes in the *Dialogue Concerning Heresies,*" *The Library* 5th series, 27 (1972): 233-35.

Doyle, A.I. "The European Circulation of Three Latin Spiritual Texts." In *Latin and Vernacular: Studies in Late-Medieval Texts and Manuscripts* [Proceedings of the 1987 York Manuscripts Conference], Alastair J. Minnis, ed. Cambridge: D.S. Brewer, 1989, pp. 129-46.

Dunn, Esther C. "John Rastell and 'Gentleness and Nobility.'" *Modern Language Review* 12 (1917): 266-78.

Erikson, Amy L. "Common Law versus Common Practice: The Use of Marriage Settlements in Early Modern England." *Economic History Review* 43 (1990): 21-39.

Geritz, Albert J. and Amos Lee Laine. *John Rastell.* Boston: Twayne Publishers, 1983.

Geritz, Albert J. "The Marriage Date of John Rastell and Elizabeth More." *Moreana* 52 (1976): 23-4

———. "Recent Studies in John Rastell." *English Literary Renaissance* 8 (1978): 341-50.

Graham, Howard Jay. "'Our Tong Maternall Maruellously Amendyd and Augmentyd': the First Englishing and Printing of the Medieval Statutes at Large, 1530-1533." *UCLA Law Review* 13 (1958): 58-98.

———. "The Rastells and the Printed English Law Book of the Renaissance." *Law Library Journal* 47 (1954): 6-25.

Graham, Howard Jay and John W. Heckel. "The Book that 'made' the Common Law: The First Printing of Fitzherbert's 'La Graunde Abridgement,' 1514-1515." *Law Library Journal* 51 (1958): 100-116.

Greer, David. "Sleepest or Wakest Thou Iolly Shepheard." *Shakespeare Quarterly* 43 (1992): 224-26.

Greg, W. W. "Notes on Some Early Plays." *The Library*, 4th series, 11 (1930): 46-50.

Hogrefe, Pearl. "The Life of Christopher Saint Germain." *Review of English Studies* 13 (1937): 398-404.

———. *The Sir Thomas More Circle: A Program of Ideas and Their Impact on Secular Drama.* Urbana: University of Illinois Press, 1959.

Isaac, Frank S. *English and Scottish Printing Types*. vol. 1: 1501-35 * 1508-41. vol. 2: 1535-58 * *1552-58*. Oxford: Oxford University Press, 1930-32.

King, Alexander Hyatt. *Four Hundred Years of Music Printing*. London: Eyre and Spottiswoode, 1964.

——. "Rastell Reunited," In *Essays in Honour of Victor Scholderer*, Dennis E. Rhodes, ed. Mainz: Karl Pressler, 1970, pp. 213-18.

——. "The Significance of John Rastell in Early Music Printing." *The Library*, 5th series, 26 (1971): 197-214.

Kinsman, Robert S. "The Printer and Date of Publication of Skelton's 'Agaynste a Comely Coystrowne' and 'Dyuers Balettys.'" *Huntington Library Quarterly* 16 (1952-53): 203-10.

Leechman, Douglas. "John Rastell and the Indians." *Queen's Quarterly* 51 (1944): 73-7.

Mullally, Robert. "The Source of the *Fulgens* Woodcut." *Theatre Notebook* 30 (1976): 61-5.

Nash, Ray. "Rastell Fragments at Dartmouth." *The Library*, 4th series, 24 (1944): 66-73.

Norland, Howard B. "*Calisto and Melebea*," chapter 17 in *Early Tudor Drama, 1485-1558*. Lincoln: University of Nebraska Press, 1995.

Nugent, Elizabeth M. "Sources of John Rastell's *The Nature of the Four Elements*." *PMLA* 57 (1942): 74-88.

Ozawa, Hiroshi. "The Structural Innovations of the More Circle Dramatists." *Shakespeare-Studies* (Tokyo), 19 (1980-81): 1-23.

Parks, George B. "Rastell and Waldseemüller's Map." *PMLA* 58 (1943): 572-4.

——. "The Geography of the *Interlude of the Four Elements*." *Philological Quarterly* 17 (1938): 251-62.

Parr, Johnstone. "John Rastell's Geographical Knowledge of America." *Philological Quarterly* 27 (1948): 229-40.

——. "More Sources of Rastell's *Interlude of the Four Elements*." *PMLA* 60 (1945): 48-58.

Pfister, M. "News from the New World—The Dialogue Between Elizabethan Poets and the Travellers." *Casa De Las Americas* 180 (1990): 96-113.

Plomer, Henry R. "John Rastell and his Contemporaries." *Bibliographica* 2 (1896): 437-51.

——. "Pleadings in a Theatrical Lawsuit. From the Records of the Court of Requests. John Rastell v. Henry Walton." In *An English Garner: Fifteenth Century Prose and Verse*, ed. Alfred W. Pollard. London: Archibald Constable and Co., 1903. Repr. New York, 1964. pp. 307-21.

Reed, Arthur W. "John Rastell, Printer, Lawyer, Venturer, Dramatist, and Controversialist," In *Early Tudor Drama: Medwall, the Rastells, Heywood, and the More Circle*. London: Methuen, 1926, pp. 1-28 [chapter 1].

Roberts, R.J. "John Rastell's Inventory of 1538," *The Library*, 6th series, 1 (1979): 34-42.

Salmon, Vivian. "John Rastell and the Normalization of Early Sixteenth Century Orthography," In *Essays on English Language in Honour of Bertil Sundby*, ed. Leiv E. Breivik, Arnoldus Hille, and Stig Johansson. Oslo: Novus, 1989, pp. 289-301.

Steele, Robert. "A Note on 'A New Interlude.'" *The Library*, 4th series, 9 (1928): 90-1.

——. *The Earliest English Music Printing: A Description and Bibliography of English Printed Music to the Close of the Sixteenth Century.* London: Chiswick Press, 1903.

Westfall, Suzanne R. "'The Actors Are Come Hither': Literary Analogues of Itinerant Player Troupe Procedures." *Theatre Survey* 30 (1989): 59-68.

Willoughby, Edwin E. "Printer's Mark of John Rastell." *Library Quarterly* 6 (1936): 420-1.

Zall, Paul M., ed. *A Hundred Merry Tales and Other English Jestbooks of the Fifteenth and Sixteenth Centuries.* Lincoln: University of Nebraska Press, 1963.